ALL IN

MAGNUS BORGERSON

NORSE MYTHOLOGY

Discover the Tales of Origin, Beliefs, & Myths in Nordic Folklore

THE EPIC SAGA OF THE GODS, GODDESSES, HEROES, AND CREATURES IN ANCIENT NORTHERN LEGENDS

BONUS INSIDE

TABLE OF CONTENTS

INTRODUCTION

In the contemporary world, Norse mythology, much like a gem obscured by dust, has often been oversimplified or misunderstood. Such misinterpretations, pushed by popular media and cultural adaptations, rob you of these ancient stories' depth and fineness. When Thor's hammer is reduced to a mere cinematic prop, or Loki's complex character is flattened into a simple villain, the Norse universe fades into the background.

As Norse legends continue to shape novels, films, and even spiritual pursuits in the current era, the urgency to truly understand them has never been more pressing. These are not just relics of the past; they are living, breathing traditions with roots that dig deep into the human psyche.

With that, traverse beyond the well-trodden tales of Odin's one-eyed wisdom or Freyja's valiant chariot. This book will serve as a bridge, reconnecting you with the authentic spirit of Norse mythology. It delves beyond the surface-level narratives to uncover these ancient sagas' cultural, spiritual, and historical roots. Explore the myths in their truest form, unmarred by contemporary misconceptions.

Drawing from my passion for medieval literature as a seasoned historian and medieval literature enthusiast, the contents of this book were researched from authentic sources, such as the Eddas and Sagas. As you turn each page, emerge not just with tales of heroes and beasts but with a comprehension of Norse mythology, a bridge that connects ancient wisdom with today's modern iterations.

Allow this book to be your gateway to delve into the philosophical underpinnings of these stories, their timeless resonance in today's world, and the interplay between humanity, nature, and the vast cosmos. With a myriad of evidence—*be it archaeological findings, historical documentation, or comparative mythological studies*—the narratives come alive in their most authentic form.

Cross the mists of Yggdrasil, face the mighty giants of Jotunheim, celebrate in the majestic halls of Asgard, and seek the cryptic messages within runes. Dive headfirst into this world, and let the sagas of old captivate your spirit with their eternal enticement.

CHAPTER 1

THE CREATION AND COSMIC STRUCTURE

Imagine a blank canvas, a world where nothing existed. An expansive void, silent and motionless. This was the beginning of the Norse universe. But like the first stroke of paint on that canvas, the universe sprang to life in vibrant splashes of myths and legends. *Have you ever wondered where the first giant came from or how the majestic realms of gods, giants, and elves are connected?*

Dive into the tales of Ymir, the primordial being, and Audhumla, the nourishing cow whose mysterious ways led to the creation of the first gods. Journey through the Nine Worlds, each a unique tapestry of stories, from the shimmering palaces of Asgard to the fiery chasms of Muspelheim. And at the heart of it all stands Yggdrasil, the World Tree, binding these realms in an eternal embrace.

The Beginning

Every great story starts somewhere. Perhaps it begins with a once-upon-a-time or a long, long time ago. *But what if the story is more than a mere fairy tale or a distant history? What if it is the origin of a whole universe?*

Grasping the dawn of Norse mythology means recounting tales and understanding the roots of a cosmic narrative. Realize that you discover the heartbeat of all that follows in these early echoes.

To truly grasp the magnitude of Norse legends, immerse yourself in its inception.

Ginnungagap

In stories, an emptiness existed before grand battles were fought or heroes were born. This emptiness was neither dark nor light nor cold nor warm. It was the epitome of neutrality, a space waiting to be filled, a canvas untouched, known as Ginnungagap, the yawning void.

Much like the silent space between two heartbeats or the peaceful pause before the first note of a symphony, Ginnungagap held within it the promise of everything yet to come. It was the space between spaces, the time before time began. In your daily life, you may have often overlooked the beauty of emptiness, mistaking it for absence. But in Norse cosmology, this void was not an absence but a potential—a place of equilibrium, the calm before the metaphorical storm of creation.

It is a challenging concept, understanding the vast importance of 'nothingness.' Yet, just as a sculptor sees potential within a block of marble or an artist finds inspiration on a blank sheet, the Norse saw Ginnungagap as the very foundation of existence.

To the north of Ginnungagap lay the Niflheim, a place of biting cold and swirling mists. In the south was Muspelheim, a land of fiery passion and unrelenting heat. These two realms, so contrasting in nature, bordered the Ginnungagap. And in this yawning void, their elemental forces would eventually meet, setting the stage for the birth of Ymir, the primordial giant, and Audhumla, the nourishing cow.

To truly appreciate the expanse of this void is to understand that every story, no matter how grand, requires a place to start. Every legend, no matter how vast, needs its foundation. Ginnungagap serves as a reminder that even quiet and unassuming beginnings hold the seeds of greatness within them.

Ymir

From the deep silence of Ginnungagap, as the elemental forces of fire from Muspelheim and icy mists from Niflheim met, emerged a being of unparalleled significance. His name was Ymir. If Ginnungagap was the canvas, Ymir was the first bold brushstroke, setting the course for the rich tales that would follow.

Imagine the awe of witnessing the birth of the very first entity, the embodiment of raw potential. Ymir was not just any creation; he was the primordial giant, the ancestor from whom all other giants would descend. But Ymir was not merely a product of his environment. In many ways, he was the environment, reflecting the raw and untamed forces that bore him. His mere presence turned the once tranquil Ginnungagap into a theater of life.

The birth of Ymir is more than an event; it is an allegory. It serves as a reminder of the unpredictability and spontaneity of life itself. Just as the unpredictable meeting of fire and ice birthed Ymir, our lives, too, are shaped by unexpected moments, encounters, and emotions. The Norse understood that creation often came from contrasts. The warmth of fire and the chill of ice, two opposing forces, produced a being that was neither wholly one nor the other but an amalgamation of both.

The tale of Ymir challenges the perceptions of beginnings. Often, people believe that great things emerge from perfect conditions. Yet, Ymir, a monumental figure in Norse mythology, arose from the chaotic meeting of two extremes. It serves as a reminder that sometimes, the most unexpected combinations can result in magnificent outcomes.

However, Ymir's significance does not stop at his birth. His existence was pivotal to the Norse understanding of the world's structure. Without giving too much away, Ymir's role in the grand scheme of things is both a testament to the cyclical nature of life and a nod to the interconnectedness of all beings. Ymir, hence, embodies nature's unpredictability, the dance of opposites, and the ever-present potential for rebirth from chaos.

Audhumla

Another wondrous birth occurred as the mighty Ymir took his first breaths amidst the elemental dance within Ginnungagap. Rising from the same magical melding of fire and ice was Audhumla, a being of a different nature but equally significant. If Ymir was the raw, unbridled force of creation, Audhumla was its nurturing heart, the gentle yet persistent rhythm echoing through the cosmos.

Audhumla was no ordinary being. She was a colossal cow, a symbol of sustenance and life in many ancient cultures. But to reduce her to just her form would be an injustice. Audhumla symbolized nature's abundance, a testament to the idea that life can nourish and sustain itself even in the most unexpected places. From her came rivers of milk, providing Ymir with sustenance. Here, in the cold vastness of Ginnungagap, was a tale of interdependence, a story of how even the mightiest of beings rely on the simple, nurturing acts of another.

As Audhumla fed Ymir, she found nourishment by licking the salty ice blocks of Ginnungagap. And as she did so, she slowly unveiled another marvel. A new figure emerged from the ice with each stroke of her massive tongue. This was Buri, the first of the Aesir gods. In this act, Audhumla was a nurturer and creator, shaping the destiny of beings and realms yet to come.

The story of Audhumla speaks volumes about the delicate balance and profound connections that define existence. It underscores the idea that every being, no matter how great or small, plays a role in the grand tapestry of life. It is a tale that reminds us of the bonds that connect all of existence, the silent threads that weave stories, lives, and destinies together.

Audhumla's significance also lies in her gentle persistence. While Ymir's creation was explosive, a testament to the fiery clash of elements, Audhumla's actions were steady and gradual. She demonstrates that creation is not always about grand gestures. Sometimes, it is the gentle, consistent acts that bring about the most profound changes. Her story is a beautiful reminder of the power of patience and the magic that can unfold when you persevere.

For the Norse, the tale of Audhumla was not just an account of origins; it was a reflection of life itself. It was a narrative that celebrated the interconnectedness of all things, the balance between giving and receiving, and the quiet power of persistence. They saw in her the rhythms of nature—the nurturing warmth of the sun, the gentle caress of the rain, and the steady embrace of the earth.

Through the tale of Audhumla, the Norse whisper the wonders of life's interplay, the dance of creation and sustenance, and the enduring magic that unfolds when you honor your connections with the world around you.

The Nine Worlds

Towering above all, with its branches stretching across the cosmos and its roots delving into the foundations of the universe, Yggdrasil stands as the ultimate symbol of connection and continuity in Norse mythology. It supports and nourishes all the Nine Worlds, acting as a conduit for their energies and interconnections.

High upon its topmost branches shimmer the leaves of Asgard, the divine home of the Aesir gods. Nestled just below, Vanaheim beckons, the realm of the enigmatic Vanir deities. Across a sturdy bough, Alfheim glitters, where the ethereal Light Elves reside.

Around the strong trunk lies Midgard, the realm of humanity, bridged to the divine by the Bifrost, a rainbow of legend. As your eyes descend, the shadows of Svartalfheim emerge, the enclave of the cunning Dwarfs, while nearby, Jotunheim stretches vast, the land of the towering Giants.

Now, as your vision plunges to the gnarled roots, deeper connections reveal themselves. Three of these roots extend with purpose, intertwining with the essence of the cosmos. One reaches the well of Urd in Asgard, where the Norns, the fates of the Norse cosmos, weave destinies. Another delves into the spring of Mimir, a reservoir of unparalleled wisdom and knowledge. The final root finds its way to Hvergelmir in Niflheim, the bubbling source from which all waters flow, marking the chilling realms. There is Niflheim, enveloped in mist and cold, juxtaposed with the fiery intensity of Muspelheim. And, in the quietest recesses, Helheim waits, the somber realm for souls on their final journey.

Knowing Yggdrasil and its nine worlds is more than understanding locations on a map. It is to embrace a worldview, a cosmic structure that binds existence, tales, and destinies.

Asgard

From the tranquil depths of Ginnungagap to the emergence of primordial entities like Ymir and Audhumla, the narrative ascends to Asgard's resplendent realm. Here lies Asgard, a celestial kingdom perched above all, ringed by vigilant walls.

Asgard transcends the notion of a mere celestial fortress. It is a confluence of bravery and intellect, where the courage of the heart melds with the wisdom of the mind. This realm is home to the Aesir, a distinguished assembly of gods and goddesses whose stories of heroism, affection, trickery, and devotion form the backbone of mythic lore.

Under the leadership of Odin, these deities do more than inhabit Asgard; they forge their fate, uphold their sanctity, and extend their influence across other realms. Grand halls like Valhalla and Vingolf, adorned in splendor, resound with the joy of deities, the chants of noble warriors, and the murmurs of timeless prophecies.

Yet, Asgard is an embodiment of contrasts. Amidst its triumphant feasts and celebrations, it remains a stronghold of erudition and strategic thought. Ever in pursuit of knowledge, Odin ponders the cosmos' enigmas, while Thor, wielding his formidable hammer, remains vigilant, safeguarding Asgard against looming dangers.

Midgard

Emerging from the celestial brilliance of Asgard, we find ourselves drawn to a realm that might feel eerily familiar. This is Midgard, a bastion of life, perched delicately between realms of divinity and chaos. Suspended amidst the cosmos, it is encircled by a vast ocean, wherein Jormungandr, the mighty sea serpent, chases its tail.

At first glance, its landscapes of rolling hills, dense forests, roaring seas, and towering mountains might remind one of Earth. And there is a reason for that; Midgard translates to *"Middle Fortress,"* representing the world of humans. It is where mortals live, love, battle, and weave their destinies.

Yet, this realm is no isolated island in the cosmic sea. It is connected to Asgard by the Bifrost, the ethereal rainbow bridge, symbolizing the profound link between gods and humans. While the inhabitants of Midgard might not wield the powers of the Aesir, their lives, choices, and fates are deeply intertwined with the divine. Heroes are born here, legends arise, and sagas that shape the very core of Norse tales unfold on this same soil.

But Midgard is not just about the human experience. Its shores, forests, and skies are home to many creatures—from majestic stags and formidable wolves to enigmatic dwarfs and elves. Their interactions with mortals add complexity and wonder to this already vibrant realm.

Vanaheim

Leaving behind the familiarity of Midgard, your journey takes you to a realm shimmering with ancient energies and mysteries. This is Vanaheim, the verdant cradle of fertility, prosperity, and peace. It is the land of the Vanir, a group of deities distinct from the Aesir of Asgard but no less influential or revered.

While Asgard resonates with tales of valor and strategic prowess, Vanaheim embodies the gentler rhythms of nature. The Vanir are gods and goddesses of the elements—of seasons, growth, and time's cyclical dance. They are not just witnesses to nature's cycles but active participants, their essence woven into every bud that blossoms and every stream that murmurs.

Njord, the sea god who calms the waves and ensures bountiful catches for fishermen, calls Vanaheim his home. His children, the radiant Freyr and the enchanting Freyja, shape the realms of fertility and love, influencing not just the land's bounty but the emotions and desires of beings across realms.

But Vanaheim's significance is not limited to its gods. This realm is a haven of balance. Here, nature's raw power meets the tranquil touch of divine wisdom. Gentle rains kiss rolling meadows, and dense woodlands echo with whispered secrets from times long past. It is a place where one can truly feel the pulse of the cosmos, where every blade of grass and drop of dew resonates with age-old magic.

Jotunheim

As you move away from the serene meadows of Vanaheim, the landscape begins to change, becoming rugged, wilder, and bearing an untamed spirit. Welcome to Jotunheim, the expansive realm of mountains, frosty expanses, and untamed wildernesses. It starkly contrasts with the orderly beauty of Vanaheim or the human touch of Midgard. This is the land of the giants, or as the Norse call them, the Jotunn.

Jotunheim is not a realm of evil, as one might expect when hearing the term *"giants."* Instead, it is a land of raw, primal power. The giants here embody nature's untamed forces—from the fierce storm to the mighty avalanche. They are not so much the villains of Norse tales but rather powerful entities with their desires, relationships, and intricacies.

At the heart of Jotunheim lies the fortress of Utgard, where many of these enigmatic beings reside. Ruled by the cunning Utgard-Loki, this fortress is a testament to the giants' might and ability to challenge even the gods of Asgard. Thor, the thunder god, often finds himself in Jotunheim, sometimes in conflict with its inhabitants and, at other times, learning from them.

While the Jotunn are powerful, they possess wisdom, wit, and knowledge. Their interactions with gods and mortals often reveal profound truths, offering insights that reshape destinies. It is a realm where strength meets intellect, the boundaries of friend and foe blur, and tales of challenges, riddles, and unexpected alliances unfold.

Alfheim

Beyond the rugged landscapes of Jotunheim, a gentle radiance beckons, leading us to a realm awash in ethereal light. This is Alfheim, a domain where every glade, brook, and breeze shimmer with a soft, otherworldly glow. Here, the air feels lighter, filled with tranquility that soothes the spirit.

Alfheim is home to the Light Elves, graceful beings known for their beauty and ethereal presence. These are not the mischievous elves of common folklore but entities of genuine grace and serenity. Moving with gentle elegance, they inhabit the land, tending to its luminous flora and nurturing the delicate harmonies of their realm.

The landscapes here are a vision of enchantment. Silver-leaved trees with golden fruits stand beside crystal-clear waters, reflecting the myriad colors of the skies above. Soft and lilting melodies drift on the breeze, creating an atmosphere of perpetual twilight magic.

For all their celestial beauty, the light elves are not mere decorations in this shimmering world. They possess profound wisdom, often aiding gods and mortals with their insights. Many a hero has ventured into Alfheim, seeking their counsel or simply basking in the realm's serene beauty.

While Alfheim might seem distant from the challenges and adventures of other realms, it holds its mysteries. Hidden groves, ancient rituals, and tales of love, artistry, and dreams are all woven into its tapestry. As you journey through its radiant meadows and under its starlit canopies, Alfheim offers a pause, a breath of luminous wonder in the vast saga of the Norse cosmos.

Svartalfheim

Descending from the shimmering serenity of Alfheim, our path takes a more enigmatic turn. The atmosphere thickens, shadows dance, and the earth seems alive with secrets. Svartalfheim, known as Nidavellir, is a realm of cavernous depths, hidden treasures, and unmatched craftsmanship. Unlike the airy beauty of Alfheim, the wonders lie beneath, in the heart of the land.

This subterranean realm is the stronghold of the Dwarfs, master smiths, and artisans renowned throughout the cosmos for their skill. These industrious beings might not have the elegance of the Light Elves or the raw power of the Jotunn, but they wield a different kind of influence: the art of creation. Their hands have forged some of the most iconic artifacts in Norse mythology. Mjölnir, Thor's mighty hammer, and even the chain that binds the formidable wolf Fenrir result from their unparalleled craftsmanship.

The land of Svartalfheim itself is a marvel. Deep tunnels lead to vast chambers illuminated by luminescent minerals. Rivers of molten metal flow, and the rhythmic sound of hammers on anvils reverberates through the stone. But it is not all fire and metal; there are also caverns filled with gems of every hue, reflecting the essence of the realm's beauty and mystery.

But the Dwarfs, while masters of their craft, are also shrewd bargainers, not ones to be trifled with. Many tales unfold where gods, in need of expertise, navigate the complexities of deals, bargains, and sometimes, deceptions.

Niflheim

From the industrious corridors of Svartalfheim, you venture into a realm where the air grows colder, and a pervasive mist begins to envelop everything. This is Niflheim, where icy winds whisper tales of ancient times, and the thick fog holds mysteries yet to be unraveled. It embodies primordial cold, a land of ice and mist, far removed from the warmth of other realms.

Niflheim is more than a barren expanse of frost and fog. Deep within its icy reaches lies the wellspring of all waters, Hvergelmir, from which countless rivers flow. It is a source of life, but paradoxically, it is nestled within a realm often associated with desolation.

And then there are the inhabitants. In this frost-laden world, creatures of ice roam, each adapted to the realm's unforgiving conditions. But none are as notable as Nidhogg, the fearsome dragon that gnaws at the roots of Yggdrasil, the World Tree. Its actions might seem destructive, but in the grand scheme of things, it plays a crucial role in the balance of life and decay.

Journeying through Niflheim is akin to stepping back to an era when the cosmos was still finding its shape, where the cold was not just a temperature but a primal force. Every snowflake, every gust of wind here carries the weight of ages.

While many tales of Norse mythology revolve around battles and valor, Niflheim offers a different narrative. Here, endurance, resilience, and the power of nature take center stage. It serves as a reminder of the cosmos's vastness, realms beyond the familiar, and the eternal dance of creation and dissolution. Within its icy embrace, Niflheim holds secrets as ancient as the cosmos, waiting for those daring enough to seek them out.

Muspelheim

From the bone-chilling expanses of Niflheim, you are suddenly thrust into an inferno of roaring flames and scorching heat. This is Muspelheim, the polar opposite of Niflheim, a realm ablaze with fire and chaos. Here, the sky is painted with vibrant streaks of orange, red, and gold, and the ground rumbles with the relentless energy of the land itself.

Muspelheim serves as the essence of creation through fire beyond its role as a place of destruction and heat. Just as Niflheim embodies the ancient cold, Muspelheim represents the primal fire that brings warmth, energy, and cosmic transformation.

Surtr, the colossal fire giant whose presence radiates power and intimidation, oversees this fiery dominion. With a flaming sword that can rival the sun's brilliance, Surtr stands as both a guardian and a harbinger of Muspelheim's fierce energy. Legends foretell his pivotal role in Ragnarok, the end of days, where he will set the world ablaze, cleansing it for a new beginning.

The landscape here is ever-changing, molded, and reshaped by the ceaseless flames. Volcanoes erupt, creating new landforms, while molten rivers carve their paths through the terrain. This constant flux is a testament to Muspelheim's nature: a realm where creation and destruction go hand in hand.

But it is not just about the raw, unbridled force. The flames of Muspelheim also represent passion, desire, and the drive to forge ahead. It is a reminder that from chaos and challenge, new opportunities can arise.

Helheim

Moving away from the blistering intensity of Muspelheim, a somber tranquility begins to take hold. The land grows quieter, and an air of finality envelops the surroundings. We have arrived in Helheim, the realm of the dead. Unlike the common depictions of underworlds in other mythologies, Helheim is not solely a place of torment or sorrow. Instead, it is a realm of reflection, rest, and the inevitable cycle of life and death.

Helheim is presided over by Hel, the enigmatic ruler whose very name has become synonymous with her domain. Born of Loki and the giantess Angrboda, she is a misunderstood figure. Hel's visage is a blend of life and death, with one side of her body vibrant and alive while the other is pale and lifeless. This duality perfectly represents her realm, a place that bridges the living and the dead.

The landscape of Helheim is varied. There are tranquil meadows where souls rest, reflecting on their lives, and darker corners where the weight of one's deeds might be felt more profoundly. Yet, it is not a place of eternal damnation. Instead, it is more of a resting point, a place where souls find respite before the next phase of their journey.

Navigating through Helheim, one might come across the massive Gjallarbru bridge guarded by the fierce maiden Modgud. This bridge serves as a passageway for souls, and the echoing Gjallarhorn can sometimes be heard, announcing the arrival of the departed.

CHAPTER 2

AESIR AND VANI

*H*ave you ever wondered where the week's name *"Wednesday"* comes from? Or why does *"Thursday"* have that particular ring to it?

Dive into the mystical realms of Norse mythology, where gods and goddesses navigate through stories of love, betrayal, and heroism. In this chapter, meet the powerful Aesir and the nature-loving Vanir, two divine clans that once warred but later found unity. From Odin, the wise Allfather with ravens as companions, to Freyja, the enchanting goddess flying with a feathered cloak, these tales have inspired poets, writers, and movie makers for centuries.

The Aesir-Vanir Juxtaposition

Before delving deeper into individual gods and their heroic exploits, unravel the Norse tapestry from its beginning. Imagine two powerful families with distinct beliefs, values, and strengths, each ruling their territories, both vying for influence in the cosmic order of things. These are the Aesir and the Vanir, two clans that form the bedrock of Norse mythology and represent power and coexistence. Understanding the essence of their ancient rivalry and eventual reconciliation, you get a clearer lens to view their tales, making every triumph or tragedy even more profound.

The Aesir

The Aesir, or Warriors of Asgard, is the more widely recognized pantheon in the Norse cosmos. They hail from the grand city of Asgard, connected to the world of men by Bifrost, the shimmering rainbow bridge. In many respects, it embodies the quintessence of power and authority. These gods are often associated with war, wisdom, and the sky. Odin, the Allfather, leads this clan with his son, Thor, by his side, wielding his mighty hammer against the giants.

The origins of the Aesir trace back to Ginnungagap. From this silent void arose the first beings, and among them were the Aesir. This group, over time, defined themselves through tales of valor, intricate politics, and the ceaseless pursuit of knowledge. Their very essence is etched with leadership, vision, and governance traits. As custodians of order, they always sought to bring structure to the sprawling worlds of Yggdrasil, the World Tree.

The Vanir

On the other hand, emanating from the fertile land of Vanaheim, the Vanir represents a different facet of divinity. Where the Aesir are fierce and commanding, the Vanir are nurturing and harmonious, deeply intertwined with the Earth's rhythms. These deities preside over aspects of fertility, prosperity, and nature. Freyr, the god of fertility, and Freyja, the goddess of love and beauty, are examples of Vanir's essence.

The Vanir's roots lie in the world's rich soils and flowing waters. Their birth is as ancient as the mountains and rivers they oversee. The Vanir gods understand the delicate balance of life. They are caretakers of growth, guardians of abundance, and masters of the land and sea. Their stories are interwoven with tales of seasonal cycles, bountiful harvests, and the ebb and flow of tides.

Differentiating Them

Though both clans may seem worlds apart in their values and dominions, their differences make the Norse Pantheon riveting. There was a time when these differences led to war, a cosmic conflict that reverberated through the nine realms.

Below are some ways to help you remember the two clans' differences.

- **Symbolic Visualization:** Create a mental or visual imagery for each clan. Think of the Aesir as majestic eagles soaring high, commanding the skies. Conversely, envision the Vanir as robust oak trees, deeply rooted in the earth, providing shelter and sustenance.
- **Mantras or Keywords:** Assign specific words to each group to quickly distinguish between them. For the Aesir, words like *"Sky," "Authority,"* and *"War"* might be apt. For the Vanir, *"Earth," "Nurturing,"* and *"Harvest"* capture their essence.
- **Use Colors:** When studying or reflecting on the two clans, associate a color with each. Perhaps silver or blue for the sky-loving Aesir and green or gold for the earthbound Vanir. These colors can serve as mnemonic devices, helping to recall each clan's core attributes.
- **Core Values Approach:** When reading their tales or myths, constantly revert to the clan's core values. *Does this story reflect power, wisdom, and leadership (Aesir) or fertility, growth, and harmony (Vanir)?*
- **Locale and Environment:** Remember their homes. Visualize Asgard's grandeur and the shimmering Bifrost, connecting it to Midgard. Contrast this with the fertile landscapes of Vanaheim, filled with lush greenery and flowing rivers.

- **Relatable Analogies:** Compare the two clans to known concepts or stories. The Aesir could be likened to the kings and warriors in a castle, while the Vanir could be seen as the farmers and sailors, deeply connected with the land and waters, essentially nature.
- **Embrace Their Duality**: Instead of seeing them as separate entities, perceive the Aesir and Vanir as two sides of the same coin. Understand that one's existence enhances the other's meaning. Reflect on how their differences enrich the Norse cosmos, like how day complements night or how sun and rain work together to nourish the earth.

Aesir Gods and Goddesses

Residing in the majestic realm of Asgard, these celestial beings, often depicted as warriors, kings, and seers, play pivotal roles in shaping the fate of mortals and upholding the cosmos' very fabric. Amidst golden halls and the melodies of skalds, these gods and goddesses dominate the lore and reflect the virtues, vices, and values integral to Viking society. Journey through Asgard's grand corridors and unveil these iconic figures' stories.

Odin (The All-Seeing Allfather of Asgard)

Within the intricate world of Norse mythology, where various beings—gods, giants, elves, and dwarves—interact and entwine, one figure stands distinct and commanding. Odin is the Aesir chief and Asgard's ruler, epitomizing wisdom, leadership, and sacrifice.

To call Odin the king of gods would be an understatement. He is the Allfather, embodying multiple roles, each as intricate and essential as the other. To those who seek knowledge, Odin becomes the epitome of the eternal student, always hungry to learn. To warriors, he is the divine strategist who imparts the wisdom of battle. And to poets and seers, he is the muse, the bringer of inspiration and foresight. Here are three stories that exemplify Odin's complexity and importance.

Odin's Sacrifice at Yggdrasil

Odin's thirst for knowledge is unparalleled. While already wise, he yearned for a deeper comprehension of the universe. This led him to Yggdrasil's roots, where waters brimming with ancient wisdom awaited.

Upon reaching the well's edge, Odin was met by Mimir, the ancient being who guarded it. Known for his unparalleled wisdom, Mimir recognized Odin's fervent desire. But the waters of the Well of Urd did not give their secrets freely. There was a price to be paid. Odin must sacrifice one of his eyes.

Imagine, for a moment, the magnitude of this choice. Odin, the Allfather, a figure of immense power and prestige, was asked to forsake a part of himself, to maim his very being, all for a sip from this enigmatic well. Yet, the weight of this decision also hinted at the immeasurable value of the well's insights.

In an act that reverberated through the Nine Realms, Odin, with a resolve that only deepened his legendary stature, plucked out one of his eyes and offered it to the well. As the eye sank into the depths, the waters stirred, accepting his sacrifice. The pain was immediate, both physical and spiritual, as Odin traded external sight for an inner vision.

This sacrifice was laden with symbolism. On one level, it represented the idea that true wisdom often demands personal sacrifice, that one must give up something precious to gain something even more invaluable. On a deeper level, it emphasized the duality of loss and gain; in losing an eye, Odin surrendered a part of his worldly vision, but in return, he gained a clarity that saw beyond the physical, that pierced through the veils of time, space, and illusion.

Through this sacrifice, Odin gained more than knowledge; he gained deep insight. He could now see the flow of fate and how the past, present, and future connected. By giving up an eye, Odin saw beyond normal limits, understanding life's depth, origins, and end.

The Military Strategist

But Odin's realm was not limited to the pursuit of wisdom. As a military strategist, he was intricately linked to the battlefield. He valued valor and bravery, and to honor the fallen heroes, he had his trusted Valkyries fly over battlefields to select the bravest warriors who had died in combat and escort them to Valhalla, Odin's grand hall in Asgard.

In Valhalla, these chosen warriors, referred to as Einherjar, were to prepare for Ragnarok, the end of days. During the day, they trained, and at night, they enjoyed feasts honoring their bravery. Their spirits were celebrated continuously. Odin, always the foresighted leader, ensured an army ready for the final battle, even as he savored the company of these worthy souls.

Huginn and Muninn

Subtler symbols often reveal deeper truths in Norse Mythology. Among these, two black ravens stand out, perched on the shoulders of Odin, their wings whispering tales from across the realms. These are Huginn and Muninn, the eyes and ears of the Allfather.

They are as telling as the tales they relay. *Huginn*, meaning *"Thought,"* and *Muninn*, meaning *"Memory,"* are not mere birds but represent fundamental aspects of Odin's psyche. They are an extension of his consciousness, soaring through the skies, venturing where even gods might hesitate.

As the first rays of sunlight break over Asgard's towering spires every dawn, Huginn and Muninn take flight. They traverse the Nine Realms, from the icy expanses of Niflheim to the fiery depths of Muspelheim, observing events, gathering tales, and witnessing the unfolding of destinies. As evening descends and shadows lengthen, they return to Odin, perching on his shoulders, recounting all they have seen and heard.

While they might be perceived as mere messengers, their roles are deeply intertwined with Odin's essence. They are reminders of the balance between thought and memory, between planning for the future and cherishing the past. Odin, despite his vast wisdom, understands the value of perspective. Through Huginn, he gains fresh insights, constantly adding to his vast reservoir of knowledge. Meanwhile, Muninn ensures that the lessons of history, the memories of ages gone by, are never forgotten.

There is a saying in Norse tales that Odin fears the loss of Muninn more than Huginn. This underscores the weight of memory and the significance of the past in shaping actions, decisions, and destinies. Forgetting one's history and roots is a fate even gods dread.

Thor (God of Thunder)

Amidst the roaring skies and echoing thunders, Thor makes his formidable presence felt. Known as the protector god, he embodies strength and valor. With a heart as vast as the oceans and a temper as fierce as a tempest, Thor represents the quintessential warrior spirit. His every tale is a testament to his insatiable urge to safeguard the realms and keep chaos at bay.

At the core of his identity lies Mjölnir, his iconic hammer. Forged by the skilled dwarf brothers Sindri *(or Brokk)* and Brokkr, this is not just a weapon but a symbol. When Thor wields Mjölnir, it signifies justice, defense, and the relentless battle against forces endangering peace and harmony beyond mere raw power.

The Birth of Mjölnir

Thor's legendary hammer, Mjölnir, was not just handed to him to satisfy your curiosity. Its creation stems from a wager steeped in deceit. Loki, the trickster god, once maliciously sheared off the hair of Sif, Thor's beloved wife. In his attempt to avoid Thor's wrath, Loki promised to gift Sif even more beautiful hair made of gold and went to the dwarves to get it made. However, Loki's scheming nature could not resist causing more mischief. He made a bet with the dwarf brothers Sindri *(or Brokk)* and Brokkr, claiming their creations could never match those of the sons of Ivaldi, another pair of talented dwarves. To make things interesting, Loki wagered his head.

As the brothers worked their forge, Loki tried to sabotage them, fearing he'd lose the bet. Despite his interference, the brothers produced three magical treasures, one of which was Mjölnir. However, Loki's meddling shortened its handle, hence its distinctive look. While the sons of Ivaldi crafted marvelous items, including Sif's new golden hair, it was deemed by the gods that Mjölnir was the most valuable of all, given its potential to defend the gods against the giants. Thus, Loki lost the bet but managed to escape in typical Loki fashion without losing his head.

Loki (The Trickster of the Aesir)

Indeed, Loki is a figure of unparalleled complexity within Norse mythology. While counted among the Aesir, his lineage is a blend of divine and elemental, as he is the son of the giant Farbauti and the goddess Laufey. This dual heritage gives him a unique position in the pantheon—neither fully god nor giant, but possessing attributes of both. This duality manifests in his actions, allegiances, and nature.

Loki's character is marked by his cunning, adaptability, and penchant for mischief. He is neither evil nor purely good but a mercurial force, bringing joy and havoc. While he aids the gods in various situations, he is also the root cause of many of their most dire predicaments.

The Tale of the Stolen Golden Hair

One of the most intriguing tales associated with Loki is the story of the theft of Sif's golden hair. Sif, the wife of Thor, was known for her beautiful, shimmering golden locks. However, one morning, she awoke to find them maliciously shorn off, with Loki being the prime suspect for this mischievous act.

The enraged Thor, upon discovering his wife's disfigurement, seizes Loki and threatens to break every bone in his body unless he makes things right. To rectify his wrong, Loki promises to provide Sif with even more splendid hair, made of real gold, that would grow just like natural hair.

Loki then descends to Svartalfheim, the realm of the dwarves known for their unparalleled craftsmanship. He approaches the sons of Ivaldi, renowned dwarf artisans, with his request. To ensure they deliver on his wish, perhaps driven by his innate love for mischief, Loki wagers his head, betting that the Ivaldi brothers could not create treasures greater than those of another pair of skilled dwarves, Brokk and Sindri.

The sons of Ivaldi not only forge a new set of golden hair for Sif but also produce two other magical items: a ship called Skidbladnir and an invulnerable spear named Gungnir. Meanwhile, Brokk and Sindri, accepting Loki's challenge, forge three other treasures, including Mjölnir and Thor's hammer *(though it turns out shorter in handle due to Loki's interference)*.

In the end, despite Loki's attempts to sabotage the contest and even though the items forged by both parties are invaluable, it is deemed that Mjölnir, with its vital importance for the defense of the gods, is the most valuable of all the items created. Thus, Brokk comes to claim Loki's head. Loki was always the cunning trickster who used a technical loophole to save his head.

But when Brokk came to claim his head as per their wager, Loki agreed but cleverly pointed out that while Brokk had a claim to his head, their bet did not grant permission to harm his neck. As a result, Brokk could not take Loki's head without damaging the neck, which was not part of their agreement.

Stymied by Loki's cunning argument but still desiring some form of recompense for the deceitful bet, Brokk decided to sew Loki's mouth shut as a form of punishment. This served as both a symbolic and literal silencing of the silver-tongued god of mischief, at least for a while.

Frigg (Goddess of marriage)

Frigg shines with a soft, radiant glow in the constellation of Aesir stars. As the Queen of the Aesir and Odin's consort, she is not just royalty in terms of lineage but, in essence too. Frigg is the epitome of wisdom, love, and motherhood. Her aura is one of warmth, foresight, and gentle power.

Often seen spinning the threads of fate with her distaff, she possesses knowledge of the future, though she never reveals it. As a mother, her love is boundless, embracing her children and every soul in the nine realms. Her tales include sacrifice, silent strength, and the unyielding power of a mother's love.

Beyond her divine duties, Frigg is also the protector of marriages and households. Many would pray to her, seeking blessings for a harmonious union or a happy home. As the goddess who understood the intricacies of relationships, Frigg, in her infinite wisdom, would bestow upon mortals the gifts of patience, understanding, and love.

In every layer of her being, Frigg embodies the multifaceted nature of femininity – she is a mother, a wife, a seer, and a leader. Through her stories, one understands the depth of her emotions, the weight of her wisdom, and the expanse of her influence. Her legacy in Norse mythology is not just that of Odin's wife but of a deity with her realm of power, compassion, and grace.

Baldr (God of Light and Beauty)

The tale of Baldr has echoed through time, touching hearts with its poignant beauty. As the god of light and purity, all beloved Baldr, a beacon of hope and joy in Asgard. His radiance was unmatched, his demeanor gentle, and his spirit kind. However, every light casts a shadow.

His tragic end, brought about by a mere mistletoe dart and orchestrated by the cunning Loki, plunged the realms into grief. The sorrow of his death was not just a personal loss; it was a cosmic one, marking the beginning of events leading to Ragnarok, the end of days. Baldr's tale is a haunting reminder of the transient nature of life and the profound impact of one life on the tapestry of the cosmos.

Lesser Known Aesir Figures

While the figures above often dominate the spotlight, the Aesir clan is vast, with each member bearing tales worth recounting.

Hodr (The Blind God)

Hodr, shrouded in the tragic shade of his blindness, is also notable for his unwitting role in one of the most poignant tales of Norse lore beyond his physical ailment. Known to many as the god who unintentionally slew his beloved brother Baldr, the repercussions of this act set the events leading to Ragnarok. Hodr's tale is a melancholic reflection of destiny's inescapable snare and the profound complexities of the gods' lives.

Tyr (God of Law and Heroic Glory)

In a pantheon filled with valorous gods, Tyr shines as an embodiment of sacrifice and bravery. Most famed for his encounter with Fenrir, Tyr displays unparalleled courage when he places his hand in the wolf's mouth as an assurance while the gods try to bind the creature. When Fenrir realizes he is tricked, he bites off Tyr's hand, marking the god's eternal reminder of sacrifice for the collective good.

Heimdall (Guardian of Bifrost)

Possessing senses so keen that he can hear grass growing on the earth and wool growing on sheep, Heimdall is the ever-watchful guardian of the Bifrost bridge. This shimmering pathway connects the world of mortals, Midgard, to the heavenly realm of Asgard. Tasked with sounding the Gjallarhorn at Ragnarok's onset, Heimdall's vigilance and loyalty to the Aesir are unwavering.

Bragi (God of Poetry and Eloquence)

Bragi, the divine personification of poetry, is a testament to the Norse culture's reverence for the spoken word and sagas. As Odin's son, he carries forth the legacy of eloquence and the magic of skaldic tradition. His body, etched with sacred runes, is both a mark of his divine heritage and a symbol of the stories and songs that form the fabric of Norse mythology.

Idunn (Goddess of Youth and Immortality)

Keeper of the enchanted apples that grant the gods their immortality, Idunn is central to the Aesir's continued vitality. Her tale becomes particularly gripping when she is kidnapped by a giant, putting all the gods at risk of aging and mortality until she is safely returned.

Vanir Gods and Goddesses

Just as the stars twinkle distinctively in the night sky, so do the luminaries of the Vanir shine in the grand cosmos of Norse mythology. Rooted deeply in the cycles of nature, the seasons' turns, and the earth's rhythms, these deities are the harmonious counterparts of the Aesir. Their tales not only enthrall with their magic and allure but also underscore the significance of balance, growth, and nurture in the grand design of existence. Set foot in Vanaheim, the lush realm of the Vanir, and acquaint yourself with its revered guardians.

Freyr (God of Fertility and Peace)

Whispers of the wind, the rustling of leaves, and the swaying of golden crops—these are but the subtle hymns that sing the praises of Freyr, the god of fertility. Revered widely as the deity who oversees growth and abundance, Freyr is a beacon of prosperity in Norse tales. With a heart attuned to the land and its creatures, he ensures bountiful harvests and peace across territories.

Freyr's Pursuit of Love

Within the annals of Norse mythology, Freyr's most celebrated tale is undeniably his courtship of the stunning jötunn, Gerðr. The story begins with Freyr, seated on Odin's throne, Hliðskjálf, where he catches a glimpse of Gerðr, so radiant that even the brightness of the sky pales in comparison. Enamored and restless, Freyr is consumed by an overwhelming desire to win her heart.

To achieve this, he sends his servant, Skírnir, as an emissary, bearing lavish gifts and promises. But Gerðr, being no easy conquest, remains unfazed. Only when Skírnir resorts to threats and a powerful enchantment does she agree to meet Freyr.

Yet, this union comes at a cost. To ensure Skírnir's assistance, Freyr parts with his cherished sword, a weapon that can fight on its own. This love-struck sacrifice not only showcases the depths of his affection for Gerðr but also preempts his vulnerable stance in the cataclysmic events of Ragnarok.

Through this tale, Freyr's character is vividly painted—a god of immeasurable power, yet susceptible to the profoundest human emotions: *love.* The intertwining of passion, sacrifice, and destiny makes this narrative one of the most memorable in Norse lore.

Magnus Borgerson

Freyja (Goddesses of Love, War, and Beauty)

Freyja is a figure of intrigue, passion, and contrasts. She embodies the many facets of womanhood. To think of her is to envision fields bathed in sunlight, lovers locked in an eternal embrace, and a mother's tender touch. Yet, Freyja's allure does not end there.

Daughter of Njord and sister to Freyr, she hails from the Vanir tribe, which is closely linked with fertility and prosperity. Her beauty is such that she has been the object of desire for many, from giants to other gods. Yet, it is her multifaceted nature that truly sets her apart. Freyja is not just the goddess of love and beauty; she is also a fierce warrior and a master of the arcane arts.

A practitioner of the mysterious seidr magic, Freyja's skills transcend typical sorcery. Seidr involves communion with the spirits, divination, and even altering one's fate—a power so profound that even Odin himself sought her tutelage to master it.

Her feathered cloak is an emblem of her freedom and power. With it, she can transform into a falcon, reaching the farthest corners of the nine realms in her flights. Whether searching for her lost husband, Óðr, or pursuing her objectives, Freyja moves with purpose and determination.

But what makes her most intriguing is her unique role in the afterlife. Unlike other deities, Freyja shares her claim over the fallen warriors with Odin. While Odin is chosen to go to Valhalla, Freyja's selected heroes are received in her hall, Sessrúmnir, located in the heavenly fields of Fólkvangr. There, amidst the serene meadows, these souls find rest and solace in the presence of the luminous goddess.

Njord (God of the Sea and Prosperity)

Amidst the vastness of the Norse pantheon, Njord stands as a serene and steadfast beacon, embodying the riches and mysteries of the sea. Revered primarily as the god of seafarers, fishing, and fertility, he resonates deeply with the coastal dwellers and anyone dependent on the sea's bounty.

Born to the Vanir, a tribe of deities associated with wealth, fertility, and the magic of nature, Njord is an emblem of abundance. The rhythmic cadence of waves, the salty breeze caressing the shorelines, and the ships returning laden with treasures—these are all under Njord's gentle dominion.

But it is not just the seas and oceans he presides over; Njord also watches over commerce and trade, ensuring prosperity for those who pay him homage. Traders and merchants often invoked his blessings for successful voyages and bountiful exchanges.

Yet, beyond his godly duties and attributes, Njord's life is interwoven with tales of love, sacrifice, and adaptation. Perhaps the most prominent is his ill-fated marriage to the mountain giantess Skadi. The two wed under peculiar circumstances: Skadi sought vengeance for her father's death, but a truce led to her marrying a god of her choice by only looking at their feet. Choosing the fairest feet, thinking they belonged to Baldr, she found herself wed to Njord instead.

Their union, however, was marked by a profound difference in lifestyles. While Njord loved the serene shores, Skadi longed for her mountainous home's snowy peaks. They tried to reconcile their differences by spending nine nights in Njord's Noatun and three in Skadi's Thrymheim. Eventually, their contrasting desires drove them apart, showcasing the challenges and compromises inherent in love and relationships.

Lesser Known Vanir Figures

Amid the vast expanses of Norse lore, while the Aesir often capture the limelight, the Vanir have unique tales to tell. These gods and goddesses, primarily associated with fertility, prosperity, and nature's magic, bring color and depth to the rich tapestry of mythology.

Nerthus (Goddess of Fertility and Earth)

Ancient and enigmatic, Nerthus is the goddess of the earth's fertility and the mysteries it harbors. Believed to be one of the oldest deities in the Vanir lineage, she was revered by early Germanic tribes. Rituals honoring her saw a sacred cart carrying her statue, which would be cleansed in a lake by enslaved people, who would then be drowned as a sacrifice to maintain the sanctity of her mysteries.

Gefjon (Goddess of Ploughing and Foreknowledge)

A beacon of strength and insight, Gefjon is famed for her cunning. Legend tells of how she tricked King Gylfi of Sweden, promising her only as much land as she could plow in one night. Transforming her four sons into oxen, she plowed out the land that would become the Danish island of Zealand. Her tale reflects the might of the Vanir's connection to the ground and their cunning in wielding it.

Kvasir (God of Inspiration)

Born from the peace treaty between the Aesir and Vanir, Kvasir was the embodiment of wisdom and knowledge. Deemed to be the wisest among gods and men, he traveled the realms, imparting wisdom. Yet, his fate was sealed when two dwarves slew him and brewed mead from his blood, granting whoever drank its poetic inspiration.

CHAPTER 3

THE WORLD OF SPIRITS AND BEINGS

Beyond the well-known gods and humans of Norse mythology lies a vast and varied landscape populated by unique spirits and beings. This chapter invites you on a journey through these lesser-known corners of the Norse world, introducing a tapestry of characters, each with its own story and significance in the larger mythological narrative.

Have you ever wondered about the colossal giants that walked the frosty realms, both foes and lovers of the gods? Or the enigmatic elves, who whispered stories of both light and shadow? And then there are the Norns, the weavers of destiny, guiding both gods and mortals alike. Not to mention the Valkyries, those fierce maiden warriors soaring across the battlefield, deciding who lives and ventures into Valhalla's great hall.

Giants

In the cradle of Norse myths, giants, or Jotunn, are awe-inspiring beings that do more than loom over the horizon. These entities are intricately woven with traits that tie them to the very fabric of nature itself. As you traverse the frosty terrains of Jotunheim, venture deeper into understanding these monumental beings' distinctive physical characteristics and temperaments.

Majestic Statures and Hues

The Jotunn are often depicted as enormous entities, with some towering over mountains while others, surprisingly, are no bigger than the average human. But their size is not the only noteworthy thing. Their physical appearances are often influenced by their dominion over nature.

For instance, a mountain Jotunn could have skin like rough granite, hair flowing like waterfalls, and eyes shining like gemstones. A frost giant would bear the colors of winter—pale blues and whites, their breath a chilly gust, and their movements echoing the silent serenity of snowfall. In stark contrast, fire giants from the fiery realms would embody the rage of volcanoes, with molten skin, eyes flickering like embers, and an aura of smoky haze.

Temperament

While their physicality is undeniably impressive, the Jotunn are far from being mere brutes. They possess a spectrum of emotions, intellect, and wisdom. Some are poets, thinkers, and even artisans, while others are warriors with a temperament as volatile as a stormy sea or as calm as a gentle brook.

Their personalities are as diverse as the landscapes they inhabit. Skadi, the aforementioned snow giantess, is fierce and independent, embodying the wild spirit of winter mountains. Thrym, on the other hand, was cunning and crafty, using wit rather than sheer strength to get what he desired.

Nature's Embodiment

A salient characteristic of the giants is their symbiotic relationship with nature. They do not merely represent natural elements; they are a part of them. This is evident in their lifecycle – as seasons change, some giants wane while others wax in strength. The spring might see the retreat of frost giants, but it heralds the rise of those connected with fertility and growth.

This bond with nature also influences their behaviors and decisions. Their actions often reflect nature's cyclic patterns: *creation, preservation,* and *destruction.* Thus, their conflicts with gods can be seen as nature's way of balancing the scales and ensuring that no single force becomes too dominant.

The Intertwined Fates of Giants and Gods

The relationship between giants and gods stands out as one of the most intricate and nuanced. To see them merely as adversaries would be akin to viewing the vastness of the Northern skies through a narrow window. Their harmonious and tumultuous ties were rooted in shared ancestry, mutual respect, love, envy, and cosmic balance's ever-present push and pull.

In understanding the ties between giants and gods, you uncover the very essence of Norse mythology: a realm where absolutes are rare and relationships are fluid. Here, enemies could become allies, lovers could hail from opposing factions, and bloodlines could merge and diverge in unexpected ways.

Alliances, Friendships, and Familial Bonds

While many stories highlight epic battles between giants and gods, emphasizing the struggle between order *(associated with the gods)* and chaos *(linked to the giants),* there is more to their relationship. Focusing only on these battles misses their numerous interactions and connections.

For example, Aegir, the ancient giant of the seas, was a revered figure known for hosting lavish feasts in his shimmering underwater halls, to which even the gods were invited. His gatherings were not mere parties but symbols of the deep-seated respect and camaraderie between certain giants and gods.

Similarly, the love story of Gerðr and Freyr defied the conventional boundaries set between their races. Gerðr, with her ethereal beauty and wisdom, enchanted Freyr, leading to a union that symbolized the harmonization of seemingly opposing forces. Their love was not just a personal bond but a testament to the possibility of unity amidst inherent differences.

For all their celestial might, the gods themselves could not deny the touch of Jotunn lineage in their ancestry. Odin, the chief of the gods and a figure of immense wisdom and power, bore the essence of giants within him. His mother, Bestla, a revered giantess, reminded him that the gods were not purely separate entities. They shared the same cosmic blood and the same ancestral roots. This blending of lineages further muddied the waters between outright enmity and kinship.

Their shared tales speak volumes about the complexities of relationships, the inevitability of conflicts, and the potential for reconciliation and unity. It serves as a powerful reminder that divisions are often superficial, and at the heart of it, all beings are intrinsically connected by the threads of fate and ancestry.

Prominent Giants

In the grand narrative of Norse mythology, the Jotunn are not mere antagonists or side characters. They are pivotal players, representing nature's raw force and myriad moods. Their appearances and characteristics are a testament to the Norse understanding of the natural world – unpredictable, diverse, and awe-inspiring. As you delve further into their tales, you will discover that these giants, with their vast statures and even vaster stories, teach you about the delicate balance of power, the rhythms of nature, and the intricate dance of chaos and order.

Thrym

Thrym's name resonates with chaos and tumult. While many giants sought power, riches, or dominance, his desires were driven by the most complex emotion of all: love. Yet, his love was not a simple or pure sentiment. It was a turbulent blend of infatuation, ambition, and cunningness, leading to one of the most audacious plots against the gods.

At the core of Thrym's bold act was his ardent longing for Freyja, whose allure was legendary even among the gods. Freyja was not just a symbol of love and fertility; she embodied beauty, allure, and power, making her a fitting object of affection for a giant who loved causing a stir. But in the vast cosmos of Norse mythology, desires rarely follow a straight path.

In fact, Thrym's intricate heist to steal Mjölnir was motivated by more than just power; it was his desperate bid to sway the scales in his favor and win Freyja's heart. Using guile, Thrym managed to get past Asgard's defenses and make off with the hammer while the gods were preoccupied. This was no spur-of-the-moment theft; it required careful planning, a deep understanding of the guards' routines, and perhaps some inside help or a distraction. By doing so, he was not merely procuring a weapon; he was making a bold statement, shifting the very dynamics of power in his favor.

Mjölnir was no ordinary weapon. It embodied Thor's power, a symbol of protection for the gods and humans alike against the forces of chaos. When Thrym laid his hands on this cosmic artifact, he was not just stealing a weapon but tilting the balance of power. With Mjölnir as his bargaining chip, Thrym thought he held all the cards. Little did he know that the gods, though momentarily taken aback, were always a step ahead. In the succeeding chapter, you will see how the gods retaliated, so stay tuned.

Skadi

Deep in the frost-covered heart of Jotunheim, where eternal winter reigns and silence is only broken by the howling winds, Skadi stood as a beacon of nature's formidable might. This was no ordinary giantess; Skadi's essence intertwined with the icy tendrils of winter itself. But within her tale, there is a journey of profound emotional depth, transcending her icy exterior, revealing passions, ambitions, and destiny intertwined with the gods.

Skadi's stature was more than just her physical presence. Her aura mirrored the unyielding, relentless force of winter. The snow-covered valleys' stillness, the north wind's biting chill, and the indomitable spirit of the arctic wolf; all these winter elements resonated in Skadi. The very mountains seemed to bow in reverence to her, acknowledging her as one of their own.

A Daughter's Vengeance

But even nature's mightiest have vulnerabilities. The core of Skadi's tale is a poignant quest for retribution. When her father, Thjazi, met a tragic end at the hands of the Aesir gods, the icy calmness that Skadi was known for transformed into a storm of rage and grief. Her determination grew with every step towards Asgard, echoing her intent to make the gods pay for their transgressions.

What began as a mission of vengeance took unexpected turns. The Aesir gods, in their wisdom, sought not confrontation but reconciliation. Through trials, challenges, and negotiations, they offered Skadi compensation for her loss. During these negotiations, an unforeseen bond blossomed between Skadi and the god Njord, the lord of the seas. It was a union of contrasts - the cold, stern realm of winter with the fluid, ever-changing domain of the oceans.

Skadi's journey, from the desolate peaks of Jotunheim to the celestial halls of Asgard, is a testament to the intricate duality of existence. Here was a being of formidable power yet driven by deeply personal emotions. Her tale underscores the idea that vengeance, love, strength, and vulnerability coexist. It serves as a poignant reminder of the depth and complexity beneath the surface, even in beings as mighty as the giants of Norse lore.

Dwarfs (The Master Artisans of the Depths)

Delving deep into the earth's bowels, the dwarfs are renowned not for their stature but for their unmatched craftsmanship. They are the unsung heroes behind some of the most potent artifacts coveted by the gods and even giants. Here is everything you need to know about them.

Origins and Habitat

Dwarfs have a profound affinity for the subterranean. Born within the embrace of stone corridors and crystalline caves, these stout beings are the spirit of the mountains. Their cities, often hidden from the prying eyes of other races, are intricate mazes of tunnels and chambers, mirroring the complexity of the dwarfs' hearts.

Appearance and Physiology

Dwarfs are typically shorter than humans, often standing between 4 to 5 feet tall. But what they lack in height, they make up for in bulk and brawn. Their broad shoulders, barrel chests, and muscular limbs testify to their life spent toiling with rock and metal.

A dwarf's visage is often marked by a thick beard, which they wear with great pride. Their eyes, deep-set beneath heavy brows, sparkle with the secrets of the earth, often reflecting the colors of precious gems they have encountered in their excavations.

Culture and Traditions

At the heart of every dwarf settlement lies the forge. It is not just a place of work but of worship. Here, amidst the dance of sparks and the rhythm of hammers, dwarfs forge more than just weapons and trinkets; they forge bonds of brotherhood and tales of their legacy.

Dwarfs revel in the joy of life. From the deep, melodious songs that echo through their caverns to the lavish feasts they host, brimming with ale and hearty meats, they cherish camaraderie and celebrate their achievements.

Craftsmanship and Artifacts

Their creations are not mere objects, but wonders imbued with magic, love, and history. Each artifact tells a story, often interwoven with enchantments that make them sought after across realms. The dwarfs are privy to many ancient techniques passed down through generations. Jealously guarded secrets allow them to craft items of unparalleled beauty and power. This expertise is why even the gods would descend from their celestial abodes to commission a piece from the masterful hands of a dwarf. From the deadly sharpness of a dwarven blade to the ethereal glow of a gem-encrusted chalice, these items are the stuff of legends.

Mjölnir

Thor, the god of thunder, with all his celestial might, wielded Mjölnir, a hammer not forged in the heavens but within the fiery depths of a dwarven forge. This artifact, a marvel of craftsmanship and magic, resonates with the clang of hammers on anvils and reverberates with the power of storms. Such is its might that with a single swing, mountains crumble, and adversaries meet their doom. This is a testament to the unparalleled skill and imagination of its dwarf creators.

Draupnir

In the silent halls of Asgard, Odin, the Allfather, wears Draupnir, a ring of pure gold. It is no ordinary trinket. The ring births eight new identical rings every ninth night in a spectacle of magic and metallurgy. This continuous multiplication displays unmatched wealth and showcases the dwarfs' profound understanding of enchantments. They did not just mold metal; they wove magic into its essence.

Relations with Other Beings

Dwarfs are inherently suspicious of outsiders. Their trust is hard-won, and betraying it can earn an enmity that lasts lifetimes. However, those who have proven themselves have found stalwart allies in dwarfs, who are as steadfast in friendship as they are in battle.

Throughout history, dwarfs have forged both rivalries and partnerships. Elves, with their love for nature and magic, often find themselves at odds with the pragmatic and earth-bound dwarfs. Yet, in times of peril, old grudges are forgotten, and the two races have been known to stand shoulder-to-shoulder against common foes.

Elves

While the dwarfs sculpt the tangible, elves are weavers of the intangible. They oversee the delicate balance between realms, ensuring the harmonious flow of energies. Much like the world's day and night, the world of elves is governed by duality. Light elves epitomize purity, benevolence, and beauty. Their ethereal glow illuminates Alfheim, and they protect all that is good and just. In stark contrast, the dark elves, dwelling in Svartalfheim, embody the shadows. Neither wholly evil nor entirely benevolent, they represent the balance necessary to maintain cosmic harmony.

Origins and Habitat

Elves hail from the ethereal planes of Alfheim, a realm where magic pulsates through every leaf and silver river flows under the gaze of opalescent moons. Alfheim, a world between realities, is a tapestry of ancient forests, shimmering glades, and lofty spires, all held together by the mystic energies the elves cherish.

Appearance and Physiology

Tall, lithe, and imbued with a grace that seems almost other-worldly, elves exude an aura of serene mystery. Their features are refined, with high cheekbones and almond-shaped eyes that hold the wisdom of the ages. Those eyes, often a clear shade of green, blue, or silver, seem to pierce through the veils of the world, seeing truths others might miss.

Their longevity is a subject of envy among many races. An elf's lifespan stretches centuries, sometimes even millennia, allowing them a vast and deep perspective.

Culture and Traditions

Magic is to elves what air is to humans. From a tender age, they are initiated into the mysteries of the arcane. Their spells, often sung in melodious voices, have the power to heal, protect, and sometimes harm.

More than just magic wielders, elves see themselves as the custodians of balance. They ensure the energies between realms remain in harmony, preventing catastrophic rifts and maintaining the order of existence.

Arts and Creations

While they may not forge weapons and armory like the dwarfs, elves are artisans in their own right. Their music can bring solace to troubled hearts or awaken memories long forgotten. Their paintings capture both sights and emotions, and their tales are woven with threads of dreams and reality.

The artifacts they produce, though fewer, are steeped in enchantments. A single elvish pendant might guide its bearer through the darkness, and a cloak woven by elven hands could render its wearer nearly invisible.

Relations with Other Beings

With their deep understanding of the interconnectedness of all things, Elves are often seen as diplomats and peacekeepers. They form alliances based on mutual respect and understanding, always seeking the path of harmony.

While their relationships with some races, like dwarfs, can be complex due to differing worldviews, elves always approach others with a desire to learn and to teach, knowing that every interaction is a step in the eternal dance of existence.

Norns

The Norns are among the most enigmatic and influential beings in Norse cosmology. As the arbiters of destiny, mortal and divine, they weave the tapestry of existence, ensuring the flow of time and events remains uninterrupted and balanced. Residing at the base of Yggdrasil, the World Tree, the Norns tend to the three main roots, drawing water from the Well of Urd to nourish it.

The Notable Norns

Few figures stand as centrally and enigmatically as the Norns. These ethereal weavers, guardians of past, present, and future, hold the threads of every being's fate, from the mightiest god to the most humble mortal. As you delve deeper into their realm, three names stand out, representing the essence of the Norns and their inexorable influence over time.

Urd

Representing what once was, Urd holds the memories of the cosmos. She understands the intricacies of events gone by, ensuring that history, both in its glory and tragedy, plays a part in shaping the future.

Verdandi

In the fleeting moment of now, Verdandi operates. She embodies the current, the real-time unfolding of events, capturing the essence of existence in its most immediate form.

Skuld

Mysterious and often elusive, Skuld holds the promise and the uncertainty of what is to come. As the guardian of tomorrow, she spins possibilities and potentialities, awaiting the dawn of each new day.

Influence on Mortal and Divine Destinies

It is often said that gods or giants cannot alter the threads woven by the Norns. Even the mighty Odin, the Allfather, seeks their counsel, understanding their unparalleled insight into the destiny of all beings.

While they weave the destiny, note that the Norns do not dictate every detail. There is a dance between fate and free will, where mortals and gods play their parts, even as the narrative remains under the Norns' domain.

Relationships with other Beings

The gods, epitomized by Odin, seek the Norns' wisdom, acknowledging their pivotal role in shaping fate. Dwarfs, master artisans of the underground, align their creations with the Norns' visions, earning their respect. Elves, through their mystic connection with nature and magic, collaborate with the Norns to maintain cosmic balance. The Jotunn, or giants, despite their conflicts with gods, are bound by prophecies crafted by these weavers of destiny. Treading the fine line between choice and preordained fate, mortals look to the Norns as guiding lights and symbols of life's inescapable trajectory.

Valkyries

The Valkyries, often visualized with gleaming armor, wings spread wide against a war-torn sky, are among the most iconic figures in Norse mythology. These supernatural maidens, whose name means *"choosers of the slain,"* serve as the bridge between mortality and divinity, between the chaos of battle and the peace of Valhalla.

Role in the Battlefield

Amid the cacophony of clashing swords and the desperate cries of warriors, the Valkyries descend, selecting the bravest of the fallen. They do not simply choose randomly; instead, they seek out those whose valor, skill, and honor shine brightest even in death's embrace.

Beyond their role as choosers, Valkyries also play an active part in determining the outcome of battles. At times, they shield favored warriors, guiding them away from death's grasp. Yet, at other moments, they might bring about the doom they later rescue souls from.

Relationship with Odin

Serving directly under Odin, the Allfather, the Valkyries are often seen as his semi-divine daughters. Their loyalty to him is unwavering, and they play a crucial role in fulfilling his vision for the great battles and the warriors who would join him in Valhalla.

In his infinite wisdom, Odin often relies on the Valkyries as gatherers of souls and as his scouts and messengers. They traverse the realms, bearing news of impending wars, shifts in power, and the murmurs of prophecy.

Bond with the Fallen

Seeing a Valkyrie was a blessing and a promise for a fallen warrior. Those chosen by these divine maidens would be whisked away to Valhalla, Odin's grand hall. Here, they would feast, recount tales of valor, and prepare for the final battle during Ragnarök.

While Valhalla was a place of honor, the transition from mortality could be jarring. In their tender grace, the Valkyries often comforted these souls, ensuring their transition was one of peace and pride. They became sisters and guides to the fallen, reminding them of their glory and the honor that awaited.

CHAPTER 4

MYTHS OF POWER AND TRIUMPH

Visualize a world where even gods are tested; power struggles lead to monumental wars, and cunning, courage, and comedy often intertwine. From a celestial war that reshaped the landscape of the gods' world to the curious events that fortified the divine city of Asgard. *And who could forget the daring escapades of Thor? Have you ever imagined the mighty thunder god in a dress?* Well, the Norse did! If you thought meeting the gods was thrilling, wait until you see them in some famous and entertaining myths.

This chapter will tackle some of the most riveting myths, such as the Aesir-Vanir War, The Myth of Asgard's Walls, The Eternal Struggle with Jormungandr, and The Enchantment of Utgard-Loki. Prepare to be immersed in a realm where every tale is a testament to the gods' mettle, wit, and occasional mischief.

The Aesir-Vanir War

The Aesir stood tall as celestial beings, reigning from the majestic realm of Asgard. To many, they were akin to the "royalty" of the divine cosmos – formidable, dignified, with eminent figures like Odin and Thor at their helm. They epitomized valor, leadership, and wisdom, often intertwined in grand tales of battle and strategy.

On the other side of this divine spectrum was the Vanir. These deities called Vanaheim their home, a realm deeply intertwined with the rhythms of nature. Their essence was the gentle caress of a summer breeze, the harmonious dance of the ocean's waves, and the burst of life that paints meadows every spring. Possessing an intrinsic connection to magic, they were especially revered for their gifts in fertility and ensuring bountiful yields.

Given their stark differences in nature and domain, it was inevitable that tensions and misunderstandings would arise between these two divine clans.

Reasons Behind the Pursuit of Peace

Diverging ideologies, contrasting domains, and innate desires often lead to confrontations among gods and their followers. Yet, amidst this tumultuous backdrop, an undercurrent of understanding beckons. Pursuing peace becomes not just a necessity but a testament to the evolved consciousness of these deities. Listed below are reasons why they want to establish peace.

- **Balance of Power:** While the Aesir and Vanir were distinct and had their strengths, they recognized the power each group held. The Aesir might have had the upper hand in warfare and leadership, but the Vanir were masters of natural magic and had unique ways of wielding influence. Neither side could claim total dominance, making an eternal war exhaustive and futile.
- **Preservation of the Cosmos:** These gods were rulers and caretakers of their realms. A prolonged conflict would not only wreak havoc among the gods but could endanger the very fabric of the universe. The Midgard *(Earth),* you know, might have suffered from their feuds, as the aftershocks of their battles had the potential to disrupt the natural order.

- **Recognition of Mutual Benefits:** Like in our world, trade and knowledge exchange are necessary. The Aesir saw value in the Vanir's skills of fertility and prosperity, which could benefit their realm. Similarly, the Vanir admired the Aesir's skills in governance and warfare. Peace meant that both sides could share resources and wisdom, leading to mutual growth.

Where It Went Wrong

With such compelling reasons to establish peace, *how did it all go south?*

The spark that ignited the war between these two divine groups was an incident involving a goddess from the Vanir named Gullveig. Representing gold and wealth, Gullveig ventured into the realm of the Aesir. However, instead of being welcomed, she was subjected to extreme hostility. The Aesir, possibly threatened or resentful of her powers, attempted to kill her by setting her aflame. Yet, Gullveig proved to be no ordinary being. After each attempt, she would resurrect, defying death three times. This act was an insult to Gullveig and the entire Vanir tribe.

Upon learning of the Æsir's actions, the Vanir were enraged. What began as a singular act of aggression against one goddess soon spiraled into a full-scale war between the two most influential groups of gods in Norse cosmology. Battles were fought, with both sides displaying immense might and magic, but neither could gain the upper hand. The Æsir, with their warlike nature and sky-bound powers, clashed with the earthy and prosperous magic of the Vanir. It was a celestial conflict, resonating through the nine realms of the Norse universe.

The Toll of War

The battles were fierce and devastating. From the walls of Asgard to the fertile fields of Vanaheim, the realms resonated with the sounds of clashing weapons and divine spells. With neither side willing to give an inch, the war raged, with victories shifting unpredictably.

In these battles, the gods showcased their unique abilities. While the Æsir displayed brute strength and battle strategies, the Vanir countered with elemental magic, calling upon the forces of nature to aid them. Tales speak of seas turning tempestuous at Njord's command and fields growing thorns to hinder Æsir warriors, all while the sky roared with Thor's thunder and lightning.

But as time passed, the toll of this divine conflict became increasingly apparent. The land, affected by the warring gods, showed signs of weariness. Harvests faltered, seas raged, and the mortal realms suffered. The realization began to dawn upon the gods that their conflict was causing irreversible damage, not just to each other but to the fabric of the cosmos.

Each day of warfare brought heart-wrenching scenes. Mighty gods, once invincible in the tales told by mortals, now bore scars, physical and emotional. The lands they oversaw suffered too. Once calm and nurturing, rivers became turbulent, and forests that once echoed with songs of life now mourned in silence.

In this chaos, a somber realization dawned upon both Aesir and Vanir. War, with all its might and glory, was an ever-consuming fire, and they were quickly running out of things to burn. With every fallen deity and every scarred piece of land, the message was clear: continue down this path, and nothing would be left but memories of a once-glorious world.

Thus, from the heart of devastation, seeds of introspection were sown. The idea of an endless battle, once filled with notions of honor and glory, is now a grim and hollow pursuit. Both clans yearned for their world's restoration, and this collective longing paved the way for peace talks. The road ahead was uncertain, but one thing was clear: the world could not withstand another divine clash.

Making Amends

In the aftermath of the tumultuous Æsir-Vanir War, a remarkable series of events took place, embodying the Norse ideals of reconciliation, integration, and the power of unity.

Hostage Exchange and the Wisdom of Mimir

To solidify their newfound alliance, the Æsir and Vanir exchanged prominent figures as tokens of trust. The Vanir sent Njord and his esteemed children, Freyr and Freyja, to reside in Asgard. In particular, Freyja's presence enriched the Æsir pantheon, as she became a leading deity linked with love, fertility, and allure. Conversely, the Æsir gave Hoenir and the wise Mimir to the Vanir. However, they were enraged with this exchange since they deemed Hoenir's decision-making lacking without Mimir's counsel. As a result, they decapitated Mimir, sending his head back to the Æsir. The Æsir, valuing Mimir's insight, preserved the lead, ensuring his wisdom remained accessible.

Birth of Kvasir

Both factions participated in a unique ritual symbolizing their commitment to peace and mutual respect. They spat into a vat, and from this mixture of divine essences arose Kvasir. Representing the pinnacle of wisdom, Kvasir was unparalleled in knowledge, an emblem of the combined strength and harmony of the now-unified gods.

Integration and Unity

The truce marked an end to hostilities and heralded an era of integration. The lines separating the Æsir and Vanir started fading, and many Vanir deities, over time, were venerated on par with the Æsir. This shift showcased the genuine integration of the two divine groups, underscoring the deep-rooted unity that had emerged from their prior discord.

The Myth of Asgard's Walls

Asgard transformed as the dust settled, and an unexpected truce was reached after the Aesir-Vanir war. Radiating divine energy and echoing the tales of Aesir gods, it represented their celestial reign and mighty legacy. Its spires shone splendor, and its halls echoed divine beings' laughter, discussions, and music. It was not just a home; Asgard was a declaration of the gods' grandeur and sovereignty in the vast cosmos.

The Need for Fortification

Yet, for all its majesty, even Asgard was not beyond peril. Giants from the frosty realm of Jotunheim were traditional adversaries of the Aesir gods. Their immense strength and occasional envy of the gods' dominion made them a persistent threat. Whispers about rumored plots, possible invasions, and potential sieges spread throughout the Nine Realms. Other malevolent beings, creatures of chaos and destruction, also cast covetous eyes upon Asgard.

The gods, in all their wisdom, recognized this. They knew their conflicts, intrigues, and battles with these formidable entities would never cease. To rely solely on their divine might during surprise attacks or sieges was a gamble they were unwilling to make. It was clear that Asgard, for all its divine aura, needed a tangible shield. A defensive measure that would stand tall against any onslaught, guarding the realm and its inhabitants from potential catastrophe. And so, the call for fortification echoed, setting the stage for events that would blend power, deception, and an unyielding quest for triumph.

The Builder's Audacious Proposal

As the Aesir gods debated on how to best fortify their celestial abode, the answer seemed to manifest from the mists of mystery. Emerging from uncharted lands, a towering stature and undeniable presence stood before them. This was no ordinary artisan; his aura bespoke of skills honed across ages and realms, and his hands bore the marks of countless wonders wrought.

His voice, deep as the abyss and resonant as ancient drums, cut through the air, *"I have constructed citadels that defy time, walls that laugh in the face of storms, and towers that touch the very stars. Grant me your trust, and Asgard shall stand unyielding against any foe."* The promise was tantalizing—an impenetrable fortress enveloping their already splendid realm. The gods, though intrigued, awaited the price for such a marvel.

But when the builder unveiled his price, it was as if a cold wind swept through the hall. He demanded not the gold of the dwarves or the melodies of elfin songs; he sought the radiant Freyja, goddess of love and beauty, to be his bride. And as if this was not audacious enough, he added a desire for the sun and the moon—the very celestial orbs that dictated the rhythm of life in the Nine Realms.

The hall erupted in murmurs. Freyja's eyes flashed with defiance and anger; the sun and moon were not mere jewels to be handed over, and the implications of their loss were unimaginable. The audacity of the proposal was clear: the builder was not just bargaining for treasures; he was challenging the essence of the gods' dominion. His demands probed deep, questioning the extent of the gods' desperation and the limits they were willing to push to ensure their security.

Loki's Cunning Challenge

In the swirl of debate and uncertainty gripping the hall of Asgard, Loki, ever the strategist, sensed an opportunity. His reputation for mischief and unpredictability was well-earned, but underneath all that was a keen mind, always analyzing and plotting. Loki's plan began to unfurl as the gods grappled with the builder's audacious demands.

Rather than dismissing the builder outright or submitting to his steep price, Loki suggested a test of the builder's confidence in his skills. The essence of his proposal was simple yet ingenious: the builder could earn his desired rewards, but only if he managed to construct the walls around Asgard during winter. And not just that; he would be restricted to using only the strength and assistance of his vaunted stallion, Svadilfari. No other aid, be it from the creatures or beings of any realm, would be permissible.

To those witnessing this challenge, it was a brilliant play. On one hand, it seemed to offer the builder a fair shot at earning his audacious demands. On the other, it set a nearly impossible task, given the enormity of the work and the tight timeline.

The builder, perhaps driven by pride or the legends of Svadilfari's unparalleled strength, saw this as not a trap but an opportunity. His confidence in accepting Loki's terms hints at his immense trust in the might of his stallion and his skills. But in this intricate strategy and high stakes, the gods knew that Loki always had an ace up his sleeve. The challenge was set, and with it, the course of events that would follow was irrevocably changed.

An Unexpected Turn of Events

With each passing day, the sheer magnitude of the builder's capabilities became evident. Under the watchful eyes of the Aesir, the walls rose from the ground as if summoned by magic, their architecture unparalleled and their foundation rock-solid. It seemed Asgard was set to have the grandest of defenses. But this rapid progress was a double-edged sword. The idea that the builder, with Svadilfari by his side, might fulfill his end of the bargain sent shivers down the gods' spines. What had initially seemed an impossible task now loomed as a reality.

However, in the shadows lurked Loki, whose cunning brain was always at work. Recognizing the gravity of the situation, he devised an audacious and risky scheme. Adopting the form of a splendid mare, Loki strutted into the construction site. Svadilfari, captivated by the allure of this mare, abandoned the builder to follow the enchanting creature into the woods. This was no mere distraction. From this unforeseen union, the cosmos would later welcome Sleipnir, a majestic steed with eight legs, destined to become one of the most revered figures in Norse lore as it will become the legendary steed of Odin.

The Confrontation

Stripped of his most valuable asset, the builder's pace came to a painful crawl. The colossal walls, once shooting up at a miraculous speed, now seemed to halt in their tracks. As time went on, it became clear that the builder, once so confident, was struggling. By the end of winter, his true identity could not be denied: he was not just an ordinary man but a giant, a long-standing enemy of the Aesir.

Upon this revelation, tensions flared. The gods felt deeply betrayed. Thunder rumbled, signaling the imminent confrontation. As the situation escalated, Thor, the protector god, stood at the forefront of the gods' response. Wielding Mjölnir, his powerful hammer, Thor confronted the deceiving giant. In defense of Asgard and to uphold the honor of the Aesir, Thor used his mighty hammer to strike down the giant, ensuring that no being, no matter how powerful, would deceive and threaten their sacred realm again.

Although the walls remained unfinished, they bore witness to the myriad tales of ambition, deceit, power, and resilience. They were not mere barriers; they were storytellers, relaying the legends of how the gods of Asgard, in their wisdom and might, defended their realm against threats, both visible and concealed. Every crevice, every stone, whispered tales of valor, making Asgard's walls a living testament to the undying spirit of the Aesir.

The Eternal Struggle with Jormungandr

In the profound, echoing depths of Midgard's vast oceans, there resided not just marine life but a creature of legend and dread: Jormungandr, the Midgard Serpent. Its gargantuan form was so massive that it effortlessly coiled worldwide, its tail meeting its mouth in an eternal loop. The very sight of this leviathan would instill fear in the hearts of mortals and immortals alike. Yet, more than its size, the prophecy associated with it kept the Asgard's gods vigilant. This ancient foretelling spoke of a cataclysmic battle between Thor, the thunder god, and Jormungandr, a fight destined to shake the foundations of the nine realms.

While their fated confrontation during Ragnarok, the end of times, was set in stone, their animosity saw several clashes before the showdown. Each encounter showcased raw power, resilience, and the unwavering spirit of a god and a beast.

One such encounter stands out, embodying the spirit of their eternal feud. Seeking to challenge and change his fate, Thor embarked on a fishing expedition unlike any other. Disguised as a mere fisherman and accompanied by the giant Hymir as his reluctant partner, Thor ventured into the very heart of the ocean. His bait was not the usual worm or fish but the head of an ox, a lure meant for a creature far from ordinary.

As expected, Jormungandr, unable to resist the offering, clamped onto the bait. And thus began an epic brawl between the protector of Asgard and the embodiment of chaos. The usually tranquil seas turned tempestuous, waves soared high, and the skies were filled with claps of thunder and bolts of lightning, mirroring Thor's determination. With grit and tenacity, he summoned all his divine might to reel in the colossal serpent.

But, as fate would have it, the culmination of this duel was snatched away. Hymir severed the fishing line, overwhelmed by fear and perhaps the realization of the prophecies. The monstrous Jormungandr, though shaken, slithered back into the abyss of Midgard's oceans, marking not the end but a mere pause in their perpetual conflict.

As tales of this monumental clash spread, it served as a poignant reminder of the relentless spirit of the gods and their eternal adversaries, forever intertwined by destiny, waiting for their ultimate battle during the twilight of the gods.

The Enchantment of Utgard-Loki

Beyond Asgard's walls and across Midgard's vast landscapes, stories of Thor's exploits resonated, from humble hearths to grand mead halls. One such tale takes us to the mysterious land of the giants, Jotunheim, and the grand hall of the enigmatic Utgard-Loki.

Eager to test his might and always searching for adventure, Thor, accompanied by his loyal friend Loki and two mortal companions, Thialfi and Roskva, set forth on a journey to this land of giants. Their quest was to showcase the might of Asgard and, perhaps, teach a lesson or two to the audacious giants.

Arriving at the castle of Utgard-Loki, the vastness of its architecture was a testament to the grandeur of giants. Every pillar resembled a towering mountain, and the ceilings resembled cloud-kissed skies. But the challenge posed by Utgard-Loki would truly test the grit of the Asgardian visitors.

In a hall filled with giants, the contests began. Loki, famed for his appetite, was put to the test of eating against a giant named Logi. To everyone's astonishment, while Loki devoured food impressively, Logi consumed the entirety of the meat, even the bones, the trencher, and everything in between! Unbeknownst to the onlookers, Logi was no ordinary giant but the embodiment of wildfire.

Next, Thialfi, renowned for his swift feet, raced against a lad named Hugi. But despite his speed, Thialfi was bested not once but thrice! It was later revealed that Hugi was the embodiment of thought, moving at a speed no one could match.

And then came Thor's challenges. First, he was tasked with emptying a drinking horn. Despite three mighty gulps, the level barely lowered. Later, he attempted to lift a gray cat from the floor, managing to raise only one of its paws after great exertion. Finally, Thor was asked to wrestle an older woman named Elli. Strangely, despite his unmatched strength, Thor was brought down to a knee by this seemingly frail opponent.

Feeling defeated and humiliated, the party prepared to leave the following day. But before their departure, Utgard-Loki unveiled the enchantments and the truths behind the challenges. The drinking horn was connected to the ocean, and Thor's gulps had caused the tides. The gray cat was none other than Jormungandr, the Midgard Serpent. And the older woman, Elli? She was old age itself, something that nothing can ever overcome.

Realizing his tests' deception and the near-apocalyptic consequences, Thor raised Mjölnir, ready to bring Utgard-Loki's hall down. But in a puff of smoke, the castle and its enigmatic owner vanished, leaving Thor and his companions in an empty plain.

Though perceived as a tale of defeat, the story of Utgard-Loki illustrates Thor's immense power and the cleverness of the giants. It is a testament to the limits of godly might when confronted by the elements of existence and nature. Yet, in Thor's ever-burning spirit, the tale also serves as a beacon of resilience and an undying quest for triumph.

CHAPTER 5

MYTHS OF BETRAYAL AND DESTINY

Imagine a world where dreams hint at the future, and every promise carries weight enough to shift the course of fate. In the heart of Norse mythology, intertwined with the tales of gods and heroes, are narratives filled with betrayal, twists of fate, and moments that test the bonds of loyalty and love.

Here, within this chapter, you delve into the poignant story of Balder, the brightest of the Aesir gods, whose destiny became tragically entangled in a plot most devious. Then, witness the strength and sacrifice in the legend of Fenrir, the fearsome wolf whose bonds were more than just chains but symbols of trust broken and the price one pays for betrayal. Finally, he journeys with Sigurd, the legendary dragon slayer whose life turns more serpentine than the dragon he sought to defeat. From treacherous kinsmen to prophecies that seal destinies, these tales serve as a reminder that even in mythology, the line between right and wrong can be as thin as the blade of a sword.

The Ominous Dreams of Balder and His Demise

Asgard, a realm usually alive with the merriment of deities, began to feel the weight of an unseen cloud. Each hall and majestic palace, usually echoing joyous tales and songs, became tinged with an air of concern. Balder was at the center of it, often described as the *"shining one,"* the god who embodied all things pure, light, and beautiful. His presence was like the first gleam of dawn after a long night or the gentle warmth felt on the skin on a sunny day. He was Asgard's radiant sun, and his distress rippled through every god, goddess, and mythical being.

Every evening, as darkness enveloped the realm, Balder's sleep was invaded. Visions of shadowy figures, sounds of mournful wails, and landscapes devoid of light tormented him. These were not just fleeting images fading with the morning light; they lingered, imprinting on Balder's soul. They were prophetic in nature, suggesting an irreversible and imminent catastrophe.

The weight of these premonitions was too heavy for Balder to bear alone. Seeking solace and understanding, he shared these unsettling dreams with his fellow gods. The mighty Odin, the wise Frigg, the thunderous Thor—all listened with growing dread. In a world where the Norns, the weavers of fate, determined the destiny of gods and mortals alike, such dreams could not be taken lightly. They were more than mere fragments of a restless mind; they were threads hinting at the future.

As the gods convened, the gravity of Balder's dreams echoed through the nine realms. The Yggdrasil, the immense tree whose roots and branches intertwined with every corner of the cosmos, sensed the gods' apprehension. Its leaves rustled with unease, and its roots trembled like the universe's foundation recognized the impending doom's magnitude.

In these moments, it became clear to the deities of Asgard that these dreams were not just Balder's burden. They were a call to all, a signal that even in the realms of gods, not everything was unyielding and eternal. The looming question remained: *Could fate be rewritten, or was Asgard on the brink of witnessing a tale steeped in sorrow and irreversible change?*

Frigg's Unyielding Promise

The weight of a mother's heart became palpable in the echoing silence of Balder's revelations. Frigg, queen of the Aesir and a beacon of wisdom and love, felt a pang that only a mother can understand. The core of her being resounded with a dread that overshadowed even the vast expanses of her divine knowledge. For Frigg, the idea of Balder's death was not just a prophecy; it was her greatest and most devastating fear come to life.

Determined to combat the looming shadows of her son's ominous dreams, Frigg resolved to take matters into her own hands. With a steely determination, she embarked on a quest unparalleled in scale and intent. Each dawn saw her venturing to the farthest corners of the universe, confronting every entity, no matter how grand or minute. From the roaring winds that raced across realms to the silent gems deep within the earth's belly, from the blinding rays of distant stars to the gentlest flutter of a butterfly's wings, Frigg approached them all. With a plea stemming from the deepest trenches of her heart, she prayed each to swear an oath: never to bring harm upon Balder.

Word of Frigg's mission spread across the realms, and such was the force of her plea, the sincerity of her tears, and the weight of her love that no entity could deny her. The seas promised never to drown Balder, the fires vowed never to scorch him, and even the creatures of fang and claw swore never to harm the beloved god.

Yet, in her exhaustive endeavors, there was but one oversight—a seemingly discreet sprig of mistletoe. It stood so tender and unassuming amidst the vast cosmos that Frigg deemed it harmless.

Who could imagine that such a delicate plant, often associated with love and festivities, could harbor any threat? It stood untouched by the vast protective web Frigg had meticulously woven, a silent and unnoticed exception amidst a universe now sworn to protect Balder.

In this fierce maternal quest, one cannot help but witness the depths of a mother's love. It is a testament to the lengths one would go to shield their beloved from any conceivable harm. Yet, the intricacies of fate are such that sometimes the most unsuspecting elements become pivotal, and in overlooking the inconspicuous, destinies are often irrevocably altered.

Loki's Web of Deceit

While Asgard rejoiced in the newfound safety of Balder, assured by Frigg's painstaking efforts, a serpent of envy and mischief slithered in its midst. Loki, often described as the wildcard amongst the Aesir, wore many masks. From playful jester to malevolent schemer, his complexities knew no bounds. While the gods celebrated their kinship and mutual admiration, Loki often stood on the fringes; his heart embittered by the affections he felt were denied.

His sharp eyes, always looking for opportunities to sow discord, did not miss the singular exemption in Frigg's vast protective spell: *the unassuming mistletoe.* In this oversight, Loki saw potential—a chance to craft a narrative of chaos and bring about the unthinkable. The mistletoe, in Loki's deft hands, underwent a dark transformation. No longer a symbol of love and celebration, it became the instrument of Asgard's impending grief.

As fate would have it, the gods, in their merriment, often amused themselves by testing Balder's newfound invulnerability, hurling weapons and elements at him, only to see them divert their course, respecting the vows made to Frigg. Unbeknownst to them, this playful act was to become the setting for a tragedy orchestrated by Loki's cunning.

Spotting Hodr, Balder's blind brother, Loki saw another pawn in his intricate game. Feigning camaraderie, he handed Hodr the deadly mistletoe arrow. The innocent, unaware, and blind Hodr, wishing to partake in the ongoing festivities, threw the arrow, with Loki subtly guiding its trajectory.

The moment that followed was one of sheer disbelief. The laughter in Asgard's halls was abruptly replaced with a stifling silence. The invincible had fallen. Balder, the beacon of light and joy, lay motionless, struck down by the thing no one had seen coming.

As tears flowed and grief engulfed Asgard, the ramifications of this act rippled through the very fabric of the cosmos. This was not just about Balder's demise, nor solely about Loki's treachery. It was a grim portent of the greater calamity awaiting the gods: the prophesied Ragnarök. Balder's fall served as a bleak reminder that destiny, no matter how diligently one tries to alter its course, has a way of asserting itself, especially when deceit and treachery cast their long shadows.

Fenrir, A Wolf Unlike Any Other

In the radiant realms of Asgard, where gods held court and heroic tales were spun, one creature's narrative grew ever more dominant, echoing with a resonance that even divine ears could not ignore. Fenrir, the great wolf, was a testament to the unpredictable nature of creation. Born of the union between Loki, the god of mischief, and Angrboda, a giantess of Jotunheim, Fenrir was an enigma wrapped in fur and fangs.

As a cub, Fenrir's innocent yips and frolics might have deceived the casual observer. His fur, pitch-black like a night without a moon, had a mystical glow. While his eyes, twin orbs of molten gold, held a mesmerizing and disconcerting depth. As days turned to nights, the cub's playful behavior was gradually overtaken by the growing power inside him. Each dawn saw him larger, more formidable, with a hunger in his gaze that seemed to grow exponentially.

In their infinite wisdom and foresight, the gods could sense the potent energy that Fenrir exuded. Once filled with tales of valor and merriment, their divine gatherings now bore an undercurrent of concern. Odin watched the wolf's movements with a furrowed brow, while even Thor, the indomitable god of thunder, treated Fenrir with cautious respect.

Whispers flitted through the golden corridors of Asgard. Tales of Fenrir's spread, not just as stories, but as cautionary tales. The wolf's howls, echoing with an eerie beauty across the realms, were a haunting reminder of his growing prowess. Gods and goddesses pondered deep questions—*could it contain such raw, intense power? Was Fenrir merely a symbol of nature's wild unpredictability, or was he a harbinger of a future chaos that could disrupt their existence?*

It was not just his physical growth that alarmed everyone. The essence of Fenrir, the very soul of the wild, posed an enigma. *How does one predict the movements of the wind or the whims of a tempest?* Fenrir, in his majestic might, had become more than just the offspring of Loki. He was nature untamed, a challenge even the gods had to reckon with, a puzzle they were now compelled to solve.

The Solution

While the courts of Asgard echoed concerns and contemplations, a decision formed in the gods' collective consciousness: Fenrir had to be bound. *But how?* Every chain, every tether they had tried, was effortlessly snapped by the wolf as if it were the flimsiest of threads. The sheer enormity of his strength became a riddle that puzzled even the most astute among the Aesir. Their efforts had to go beyond physical strength; they needed to explore the mystical world of magic and enchantment.

The answer lay deep within the darkened caverns of Svartalfheim, the realm of the dwarves. Though often overlooked in tales dominated by gods and giants, these small beings held secrets unknown to many. Their expertise in crafting was not only about working with metals but also about blending the mystical with the physical. If a solution existed, the gods believed it would be found in these underground artisans' skilled hands and ingenious minds.

Commissioned with a task that would challenge their unparalleled skills, the dwarves delved into their ancient books, whispered incantations forgotten by time and set about creating a masterpiece. They sought ingredients not from the tangible world but from the mystical, the uncommon, and the intangible. With great attention to detail, they blended these unlikely components. The outcome was Gleipnir—seemingly delicate in its appearance, but in truth, a symbol of immense strength.

Holding the silky tether, many gods expressed doubts. *Could such a fragile-looking thread restrain the mighty Fenrir?* Yet, this was the dwarves' brilliance. They had tapped into the essence of the universe, realizing that sometimes the most formidable strength is not in what is seen or felt but in what lies beneath and unseen.

Yet, the true challenge lay ahead. Crafting Gleipnir was one thing, but placing it around the massive neck of a distrusting wolf, aware of the gods' previous attempts to bind him, was another. And this endeavor would demand strength or wit and a sacrifice that would forever resonate in the annals of Norse mythology.

The Ultimate Test

Yet, amidst the towering figures of gods and goddesses, one stepped forward with a conviction that was both humbling and heroic. Tyr, the god of law and warrior justice, bore an unyielding sense of honor. He saw beyond the immediate peril, understanding that the essence of this challenge was not just about binding Fenrir but also about restoring the fragile balance that the wolf's presence had disrupted.

So, as the gods proposed their game to Fenrir—a playful challenge to test the strength of Gleipnir—the wolf's amber eyes flickered with suspicion. While Fenrir's strength was unmatched, he was also intelligent. He noticed the gods' discomfort, glances, and forced smiles. His condition—that a god put their hand in his mouth as a guarantee—was both a challenge and a declaration. He showed them he understood the stakes, emphasizing that he was no mere pawn to be played with.

A heavy silence settled. The gods looked at each other, unsure, each considering the risk. In this tense moment, Tyr bravely stepped forward, offering his hand as a guarantee. Through this act, Tyr exemplified true sacrifice, recognizing that the greater good sometimes requires personal loss.

As Gleipnir wrapped around Fenrir, its magic became evident. The chain, light as a feather, seemed to absorb Fenrir's strength, turning it against him. Each struggle, each snarl, only made the binding more unyielding. The realization of betrayal dawned on Fenrir, and in that moment of enraged clarity, he bit down, claiming Tyr's hand.

The meadows of Asgard, which had witnessed countless tales of bravery, saw a different kind of heroism that day. It was a tale of sacrifice and honor, of a god who gave up a part of himself to ensure the safety of all. Tyr's loss became a symbol, a poignant reminder that true valor often lay not in victory but in the sacrifices made along the way.

CHAPTER 6

RAGNAROK

*H*ave you ever felt the weight of an ending? The deep sense that something monumental is coming to a close? For Norse myths, that is the Ragnarok. It is an explosive battle that marks the end of the world and the creation of a new one. The term can be translated as *"fate of the gods"* or *"doom of the powers,"* it signifies the ultimate reckoning between the gods and their enemies, the giants and monsters.

In discussions of *"apocalyptic"* tales, one might envision chaotic landscapes and heroes making their final stand. But Ragnarok is unique. Even the gods knew that their days were numbered. It is where the very threads of fate have already woven the inescapable destiny of every being. As the winds of change howl and the ground trembles, the inevitable end approaches. But, like all great tales, this finale has a twist. For even in destruction, there is hope.

Delve into this chapter to explore the harrowing signs that foreshadow this cosmic showdown: The chilling prophecies of the Volva, the bone-chilling Fimbulwinter that blankets the realm, and the critical moments that push the gods, giants, and men towards their final confrontation. The air fills with the deafening blast of Heimdall's horn, signaling the breaking of the Bifrost, the rainbow bridge connecting the worlds. As the stage is set for this divine battle, witness the legendary confrontations—Odin's desperate struggle against the monstrous wolf Fenrir and Thor's fierce clash with the huge serpent Jormungandr. Yet, beyond the destruction and despair, a new dawn awaits. Uncover the rebirth, the spark of hope, and the promise of a world reborn from the ashes.

The Prelude to Ragnarok

As you venture closer to the event horizon of Norse mythology's ultimate climax, take a step back and revisit the chain of events that guided you here. Each of these moments, some grand and others intimate, wove together into a tapestry foretelling Ragnarok. Here is a concise summation:

Loki's Seeds of Discord

With a silver tongue and a penchant for chaos, the trickster Loki sired children who would become nightmares for the gods. Fenrir, the monstrous wolf, bound in chains; Jormungandr, the serpent whose vastness encircled Midgard, its tail in its mouth; and Hel, ruling over the forlorn souls in her namesake realm. Their tales were not just of birth and banishment but of a burning promise of revenge against those who confined them.

Balder's Fall

Amidst the festivities in Asgard, a shadow was cast. Balder, radiant and adored, met a fate no one had imagined. Through Loki's cunningness, the god of light was lost, plunging the realms into a sorrow so deep that even the stones wept. Balder's fall was more than a personal tragedy; it was a grim omen echoing the gods' vulnerability.

Loki's Bitter Chains

Retribution found Loki, but it was not swift. In a cave's chilling embrace, he lay bound, serpent venom dripping onto his brow. Each agonizing drop was a reminder of his deeds. And every tremor from his writhing anguish was felt as tremors across the world. Far from breaking his spirit, this torment only fanned the flames of his hatred.

Brooding Tensions and Alliances

Throughout time, even gods were not immune to conflicts of interest and ideology. The Aesir and the Vanir, two factions of divinity, had their tussles and treaties. But underlying those superficial reconciliations were deeper tensions, intensified by the grievances of the giants. These strained relationships were the undercurrents, gradually steering the world toward its prophesized fate.

Signs and Omens Leading to the End Times

As with any great saga, the approach of Ragnarok is heralded by signs, foreboding signals foretelling the end of days. These are not mere coincidences but markers indicating a cosmic shift, a universal reckoning. The world does not just tumble into chaos; it is pushed, inch by inch, through these omens that slowly but surely tilt the balance. They served as preludes, reminders that even in a world of gods and giants, there was a higher order, a destiny that even the mightiest could not evade. It was a lesson in humility and respect for the greater forces at play and a call to prepare for the twilight of the gods.

But Ragnarok does not begin with deafening roars or cataclysmic events. Instead, it starts with subtleties, with things amiss. There are betrayals among gods and kin. Brotherhoods shatter, oaths are broken, and it becomes clear that the bonds once believed unbreakable are starting to fray.

Below are other events that hinted at the coming of Ragnarok.

The Cosmic Disturbances

The cosmos offered the earliest warnings before anything took a tangible form on Earth. The once-predictable patterns of stars began to falter. Eclipses, both lunar and solar, occurred without warning. The night sky, a comforting blanket of con-stellations known to the Nordic people, started showing irreg-ularities. These cosmic disturbances were clear indicators of those who gazed upwards, a universal sign that a significant shift was on the horizon.

The Restlessness of Nature

Nature, deeply revered and intrinsically connected to the Nordic way of life, began to behave unpredictably. Seas became more turbulent without reason, with waves crashing angrily against the shores. Trees, once firm and rooted, swayed as if in discom-fort. Animals, particularly those considered sacred in Norse leg-ends, exhibited unusual behavior. Birds changed their migration patterns, and wolves, often seen in packs, roamed solitarily. The essence of the natural world seemed to be in turmoil, echoing the unrest brewing.

Unnatural Weather Patterns

Distinct from the devastating Fimbulwinter, the earlier weather anomalies were subtler. Some summers felt too short, and springs did not blossom as they should. Instead of its rhythmic fall, rain came in torrential downpours or not at all. Fog would blanket regions known for their clarity, and unexplained cold snaps would grip the warmest of lands. While not catastrophic, these weather patterns were clear deviations from the norm, underscoring the impending imbalance.

Visions and Dreams

The Nordic people placed considerable importance on dreams and visions. They were a bridge to the ethereal, a connection to the divine, a way to tap into the larger cosmic narrative that wove the fates of gods and mortals alike. As Ragnarok loomed, this dreamscape began to resonate, vividly painting the upcoming turmoil and transformation.

The All-Seeing Volva

Central to the world of Norse prophetic visions was the Volva, a powerful seeress steeped in the ancient arts of divination. The Volva, deeply connected to runes and rituals, could gain insights from cosmic sources. As the Ragnarok neared, her predictions became more potent and were filled with visions of the final days.

She spoke of a world engulfed in flames, gods meeting their destiny, the earth submerged in water, and a darkness that would swallow the sun. While deeply metaphorical, her prophecies mirrored the dreams of many, lending a weighty validation to their nocturnal visions.

Symbols and Motifs

While the Volva's words were revered, what made the premonitions of Ragnarok even more chilling was their widespread nature. It was not just the seers and shamans who dreamt of the end but the entire Norse society. Warriors, often stoic and unshakeable, reported dreams where their swords shattered against unseen forces. Farmers, usually blessed with dreams of bountiful harvests, now envisioned barren lands and withering crops. Children, whose dreams were typically free from the burdens of reality, woke up in tears, describing visions of darkened skies and a world in disarray.

Interwoven into these dreams were recurring symbols, each a puzzle piece to the larger picture of Ragnarok. There was the ship Naglfar, crafted from the nails of the dead, sailing with an army of chaos. The chained wolf, Fenrir, breaks free, its jaws stretching wide to consume the world. Serpents rising from the depths and eagles screaming their war cries. And at the center of it all, the ever-present Yggdrasil, the World Tree, its branches quivering, signaling the impending collision of realms.

Fimbulwinter and Moral Decay

Imagine the coldest winter you have ever experienced. Now, imagine that winter stretching on and on for three unending years. This is Fimbulwinter, a time in Norse tales when the world is wrapped in a never-ending freeze. But it is not only about the cold weather. This long winter is a signal, a warning of tough times ahead. Occurring before the great battle of Ragnarök, this harsh, prolonged winter symbolizes society's decaying moral fabric.

With Fimbulwinter, something strange happens. It is not just the lands that freeze; people's hearts also seem cold. Family members, who should love and care for each other, argue and fight. Brothers, who once played together, now become enemies. It is as if the world forgets about kindness and trust.

Long-standing rules and traditions that kept societies together begin to fall apart. People do not trust one another, and there is doubt everywhere. It becomes hard to find genuine friendship or love during this time. Instead of warm hugs and shared stories by the fire, people become distant, lost in the cold inside and out.

So, Fimbulwinter is more than a chilly season. It is a time when the world changes, when people forget what is truly important, like love, trust, and togetherness. And this deep freeze, both of the weather and heart, is a sign that big challenges are coming for everyone.

The Final Battle

In the intricate tales of Norse mythology filled with heroics, love, betrayal, and revenge, a climactic event stands above the rest. This moment, foreseen by prophets and deeply ingrained in the universe, determines the fate of gods and men. It is more than just a battle; it is a pivotal point that questions the very nature of life and the cosmos. Enter the ultimate showdown, marking the creation of legends and the end of eras: The Final Battle. It starts with Heimdall' blowing of horn and breaking of Bifrost, which signaled the start of two prominent confrontations.

Heimdall's Horn and the Breaking of Bifrost

Nestled within the great expanse of the cosmos lies the Bifrost, a bridge unlike any other. Radiating colors beyond mortal comprehension, it stretches as a testament to the marvels and boundaries of creation. It is not only a mere architectural wonder but a symbol, a connection. One end of this shimmering bridge touches Midgard, the realm humans call home, while the other finds its place in the celestial abode of Asgard, where gods ponder, plan, and preside.

Heimdall, with eyes as keen as the falcon's and ears that can hear the softest whisper of the grass growing, is the guardian of this bridge.

He requires less sleep than a bird and can see for a hundred leagues, whether night or day. With such attributes, he stands as the perfect sentry, alert to any disturbance, any threat to the realms.

Yet, with all his heightened senses, even Heimdall knows the weight of prophecy. There is one sound, one event, that even he dreads: the blowing of the Gjallarhorn. A horn so powerful, its call is not just a sound but a sonic force, an announcement. And as the tales of old forewarned, when its deep, resonating notes fill the air, it signals the culmination of destinies, the arrival of Ragnarok.

When Heimdall finally places the Gjallarhorn to his lips, its mournful cry tears through the fabric of all realms. A cry so potent that the very foundation of Bifrost, which had for ages withstood challenges, begins to crack, to fragment. Those rainbow hues, which once stood as a testament to unity and connection, falter and fade. The symbol of unity between the realms shatters, and the pathway between gods and men collapses.

What follows this pivotal moment is not just the absence of a bridge but a void, an unsettling realization that the safety nets are gone. The realms, which once existed in a delicate balance, held together by the Bifrost, now drift apart, isolated. This fracture is not merely physical; it is symbolic. The breaking of Bifrost signifies a shattered bond, the onset of an age of chaos where destinies collide and the world braces for its twilight.

Key Confrontations

As the Bifrost crumbles and the boundaries collapse, all entities, be they gods, giants, or monsters, heed the clarion call to arms. The fields of Vigrid become the grand stage for this cosmic confrontation, a vast plain where destinies intertwine, and ancient scores are settled.

Odin vs. Fenrir

Amidst the cataclysm of Ragnarok, where the very fabric of existence seemed to quake and shatter, a particular duel stood out, resonating with the weight of ages and the intertwined fates of its participants. This was no mere skirmish but a dance of titans, foretold since the early days of the cosmos.

Odin, the chief of the Aesir and the architect of Asgard's grandeur was a god of war and a deity of profound wisdom. He had long sought to understand and, if possible, alter the course of destiny. Raven-flanked and draped in his familiar cloak, he entered the battlefield, not with arrogance but with a sober understanding of the gravity of the prophecy he was about to face. His spear, Gungnir, gripped tightly in his hand, had seen many battles but none as monumental as this.

Fenrir emerged from the other side, breaking free from the chains that once held him. This colossal wolf, with fur as dark as the night and eyes burning with the fires of vengeance, symbolized the gods' fears and actions to contain the uncontrollable. As a pup, the gods had played with him, but as he grew, so did their apprehension. Deceitfully bound by the Aesir with the magical Gleipnir, his trust was betrayed, and a sword was wedged in his jaws to keep them open. Now, that very sword had been cast aside, and his howls echoed the pain and betrayal he had endured.

The Confrontation of Epochs

As the two adversaries faced off, the tension was palpable. Here was Odin, representing order, wisdom, and the endeavors of the gods to shape their destinies. Opposite him is Fenrir, the embodiment of chaos, wild power, and the consequences of the gods' actions.

Their battle was epic. Moving with purpose and strategy, Odin attempted to use his vast experience and the powers of Gungnir to subdue the beast. But Fenrir, driven by primal rage and the raw might that comes with it, lunged, snapped, and swirled, often making the ground tremble. Their shadows danced across the battlefield, depicting desperation and determination.

It was not just about survival. For Odin, this culminated all his efforts to protect his kin and realm. For Fenrir, it was the moment to unleash all the anguish and rage from his unjust confinement. The two forces clashed, reminding all of the fragile balance between order and chaos and the price of actions taken in fear and deceit.

Thor vs. Jormungandr

In the backdrop of Ragnarok's chaos, where the fate of realms hung precariously in the balance, a storm unlike any other brewed. This was the climax of a rivalry etched in the annals of mythology, a duel where the very elements of nature seemed to be at war.

A silhouette against the stormy sky, Thor, the god of thunder, stood resolute. His red hair, typically untamed, was tossed by the wind, reflecting the chaos. He held Mjölnir, his trusted hammer, steadily. For Thor, this was not just a fight but about protecting what he cherished most. The fate of Midgard hung in the balance, and he was its determined guardian.

From the frothing seas emerged a terror that had long been a part of the world's fabric. Jormungandr, the Midgard Serpent, was an entity of inconceivable size, having once wrapped itself around the earth's circumference. Its glistening and cold scales reflected the abyss from which it hailed. Each time it moved, waves roared, and tides surged, a testament to its unimaginable power.

The Elemental Showdown

The skies darkened as Thor took the first move, hurling Mjölnir with all his might. The impact of the hammer against the serpent sent shockwaves, with lightning bolts illuminating the monstrous creature's vast form. But Jormungandr was far from defeated. With every strike Thor delivered, the serpent retaliated, its enormous body moving with surprising agility, attempting to trap the thunder god in its coils.

It was a spectacle of nature's fury. Thunder roared, challenging the deafening hisses of the serpent. Every flash of lightning was met with a jet of venom, each drop capable of wreaking devastation.

But their duel was symbolic beyond the physical blows and the elemental onslaught. Thor, representing the bastions of order, protection, and courage, was pitted against Jormungandr's chaos, vastness, and the inescapable cycles of nature.

The Many Battles of Ragnarök

While Odin and Thor's confrontations during Ragnarök are among the most iconic, the event was marked by several other intense clashes, leading to the demise of many gods:

- **Freyr vs. Surtr:** Freyr, the god of fertility, weather, and prosperity, confronted Surtr, the infernal giant from Muspelheim. Deprived of his mighty sword, which he had previously traded for love, Freyr battled with all his might. However, his handicap was too great. After being defeated by Surtr, the giant set the world ablaze, defeating all the gods.
- **Tyr vs. Garm:** Tyr, the god of war and justice, went head-to-head with Garm, the blood-streaked hound guarding the gates of Hel. Both combatants fought fiercely, and in the end, the god and the beast perished at each other's hands.

- **Loki vs. Heimdall:** Loki, the trickster god, and Heimdall, the vigilant guardian of Bifrost, had a longstanding animosity. As fate would have it, the two met on the battlegrounds of Ragnarök. Their duel was intense, a manifestation of their mutual disdain, and ultimately, they ended each other's lives, bringing their saga to a tragic close.
- **Frigg and the Vanir:** While the precise details of their roles during Ragnarök vary between sources, many other gods and goddesses, including Frigg, Odin's wife, and members of the Vanir tribe, took part in various capacities. Many faced insurmountable odds, and the onslaught led to the death of several deities.

The Rebirth

In the shadow of Ragnarok's chaos, where the very essence of existence seemed imperiled, a glimmer of hope, faint but undying, persisted. Though scarred and shattered, the realms were not left to eternal darkness. Just as night gives way to day, from the darkest times arose a bright new beginning. This marked the rebirth in Norse mythology, where something new and vibrant emerged from the old's destruction. This was the rebirth,

Post-Ragnarok, the landscape was barely recognizable. Where once stood mighty palaces and vast forests now lay ruins and remnants. However, this devastation was not the end; it was a canvas, bare and waiting for the brushstrokes of revival. Slowly, the earth began to heal. Verdant meadows sprouted, rivers found their courses, and the sky, once bloodied and darkened, cleared to reveal its azure expanse.

What happened was the following:

Gods

While many gods fell during the great battle, some survived, carrying forth the legacy of their predecessors and the hope for a brighter future. Among these torchbearers were Odin's sons, Vidar and Vali. They had witnessed the sacrifices, the valor, and the losses and were now entrusted with the task of rebuilding. Alongside them were Thor's sons, Modi and Magni, who inherited their father's mighty hammer, Mjölnir, a symbol of resilience and strength.

Other notable survivors included Hodr, once tricked into causing Balder's demise, and Balder, who returned from Hel's domain. Their reunion, steeped in forgiveness and renewal, was emblematic of the fresh start the gods were embracing.

Lif and Lifthrasir

But the gods were not the sole bearers of the future. In the protective embrace of Yggdrasil, a human pair had remained shielded from Ragnarok's devastation. Lif and Lifthrasir, whose names symbolized *"life"* and the *"vitality of life,"* were destined to repopulate Midgard. Emerging from their sanctuary, they found a world drastically different yet filled with possibilities.

Their journey was discovering sustenance in the dew-drenched morning grass and carving out a new existence amidst the echoes of the past. In their story, the resilience and spirit of humanity shone through. New generations would spring forth from them, ensuring that the old world's tales, teachings, and legacies would not be forgotten.

The New World

As the new world began taking shape, it was not merely replicating what it once was. The tales of valor, of sacrifices made during Ragnarok, became legends told to inspire. The lessons from past mistakes, treacheries, and misunderstandings were etched in memory, guiding a more harmonious existence.

The rebirth is not only a repopulation or reconstruction. It was about reimagining and understanding the cyclical nature of existence—that there is a beginning after every end and that in the aftermath of the gravest of tragedies, life finds a way in its myriad forms.

In this reborn world, gods and humans alike embarked on physical rebuilding and spiritual rediscovery journeys. They sought to establish connections, to mend broken bonds, and to weave a tapestry rich in new tales, dreams, and aspirations.

This rebirth, rising from Ragnarok's embers, is a testament to the indomitable spirit of life itself – its ability to endure, evolve, and eternally flourish.

CHAPTER 7

RITES, RITUALS, AND NORSE DAILY LIFE

In the icy realms of the North, where myths intertwined with reality, the Vikings weaved a complex tapestry of rituals, beliefs, and traditions. Here, within the pages of this chapter, you will delve deep into the heart of Norse daily life.

Discover the sacredness of their religious practices, where ceremonies like blót and sumbel are more than mere traditions as they are profound expressions of faith and community. Venture into the mysterious realms of the Norse afterlife—*what did it take to dine beside Odin in Valhalla? Or to find oneself in the cold grip of Hel?* Unravel the criteria for these fates and immerse yourself in the profound beliefs of rebirth and the protective familial spirits that watched over each Viking household.

As the journey unfolds, witness the magic of runes, *ancient symbols of power* and *divination*. From the intricate symbols of the Elder Futhark to the art of rune casting, you are about to step into a world where every sign, symbol, and ritual holds a story, a purpose, and a heartbeat.

Religious Practices and Beliefs

Intertwined with the gods' grand sagas was the essence of their daily existence, deeply imbued with spirituality. Every whisper of the wind, rustle of leaves, or crash of waves was a dialogue with the divine. Enter the world of blót and sumbel, where the line between the mortal and the divine blurred, where offerings and toasts were a lifeline connecting the Norse to the cosmos.

Blót

The Blot is a significant ritual in the Asatru faith, serving as a method of offering to the Gods. Historically, this involved a feast with an animal dedicated and then sacrificed to the Gods. Modern practices have evolved, reflecting contemporary lifestyles. Instead of animal sacrifices, it is common today to offer mead or another alcoholic beverage to the deities as a symbolic gesture.

There is a misplaced perception about rituals labeled as *"sacrifices."* Some view them through a prism of negativity, attributing distorted interpretations from post-Pagan interpretations, intent on diminishing or mocking these practices. The idea that sacrifices are a transactional act—akin to appeasing a deity to prevent calamities—is a misconstrued notion. Likewise, the misbelief that ritual sacrifices aim to harness energy from the fear or pain of the sacrificed animal is incorrect. Sacrificing an animal was a sacred method of providing food, akin to inviting a cherished guest for a meal. The bounty from this feast was symbolically shared with the Gods.

The Asatru faith promotes a unique understanding of humanity's connection with the Gods. According to Asatru beliefs and the Eddas, humans are not just followers but are spiritually and, to some extent, physically related to the Gods. This connection is illustrated in tales like the one where the God Rig, believed to be Heimdall, fathered the human race during his visits to various farmsteads. As descendants of the Gods, humans possess *"ond,"* or the gift of ecstasy, a divine force setting them apart from other creatures. This special bond with the Gods means the Blot is not about appeasement but celebrating shared joys.

Ancient cultures valued sharing and gifting, imbuing them with magical significance. Leaders maintained a symbiotic relationship with their followers; generosity was reciprocated with loyalty. Among the Norse, a commendable leader was dubbed a *"Ring Giver,"* denoting this reciprocal relationship. The rune, named Gebo G, embodies this concept. Represented as two intersecting lines, it stands for mutual giving in relationships.

Procedures of a Blot

Performing a Blot can range from simply pouring mead as a tribute to incorporating it within a more elaborate ritual. Drawing a parallel, think of the Catholic Mass—it can be a standalone act or part of a significant event. The Blot ritual primarily involves three stages: consecration of the offering, distribution of the offering, and finally, the libation. While the ritual specifics can be intricate, involving mead, chalices, and ceremonial objects, the underlying idea is to invoke, share, and offer.

Sumbel

Where blót symbolized deep-rooted offerings, sumbel was the heartbeat of celebration and community in Norse culture. Think of it as an ode to life's moments—big and small. Envision warm, firelit longhouses, where the flickering flames cast long shadows and illuminated eager faces. Here, kin and comrades congregated, passing around a meticulously crafted horn brimming with the golden hues of mead.

But Sumbel was not just about drinking. It was an orchestrated dance of words and emotions. Participants would rise, one by one, toasting to gods, extolling their feats, or making solemn vows for the future. Each sip from the horn was not merely about quenching thirst. It was an act charged with reverence. With the rich mead flowing down their throats, they did not just drink; they imbibed the essence of their beliefs, memories, and collective spirit.

Foremost in these toasts was Odin, the Allfather, whose wisdom and might were legendary. But as the horn made its rounds, other gods, ancestors, and even tales of recent heroics were invoked. Through Sumbel, bonds were reaffirmed, memories were honored, and the intricate web of Norse society was continuously woven, ensuring that their shared history and values would endure through the ages.

Seasonal Celebrations and Festivals

The Norse calendar was interwoven with festivals marking the changing seasons. Such festivals were not just merriment but were also deeply spiritual occasions, giving thanks to the gods for harvests, seeking blessings for the coming seasons, and paying homage to ancestors. Listed below are the most celebrated festivals and events in Nordic Traditions.

Yule

Arguably the most renowned of Norse festivals, Yule heralded the midwinter solstice. As days grew shorter and nights longer, this festival was a beacon of hope, marking the anticipated return of the sun. Bonfires would pierce the long nights, symbolizing the sun's enduring light amidst the encroaching darkness. Homes were decorated with evergreen branches, a nod to life's persistence even in the harshest winter. Feasts were abundant, with families coming together to share meals, sing songs, and exchange gifts. But it was not just a mere celebration; together, they hoped and wished for the sun to reclaim its prominence.

Ostara

Aligned with the vernal equinox, Ostara was a tribute to the rejuvenation brought about by spring. Named after Eostre, a goddess associated with dawn and fertility, this festival celebrated new beginnings. As snow receded, revealing budding flora, the Norse held feasts and processions, often with symbols of fertility like eggs and hares, hoping for a fruitful year ahead.

Midsummer

Midsummer in some Nordic areas was when the sun hardly set, making it a special time full of daylight. People believed that the borders between different worlds were very thin during this time. Bonfires, lit to keep away bad spirits and hope for a good harvest, were a big part of the celebration. People also danced, ate, and had fun under the bright midnight sun, making it a lively festival.

Norse Beliefs on Soul

Within Norse cosmology, the soul was not simply a singular entity but a complex combination of aspects, each serving a distinct function in defining an individual. This idea presents a nuanced perspective on Norse identity and how one relates to the universe, the gods, and their lineage.

- **Hamr**: This was the outer layer, the corporeal essence that defined an individual's physical appearance. It is fascinating to consider that, unlike the static notion of appearance in many other cultures, the Norse believed the Hamr to be mutable. Legends of warriors transforming into animals or tales of the dead appearing paler indicate this belief. The fluidity of Hamr also underscores the Norse perspective on the transient nature of life.

- **Hugr:** At the heart of every Norse individual was the Hugr, their inherent character or essence. This was not simply a fleeting disposition or mood but the very core of their being. Postmortem, while the body decomposed, the Hugr persisted, journeying into the unknown, possibly melding with the spirit of kin yet to be born.

- **Fylgja:** Every Norse person had a spiritual counterpart, a totemic entity that resonated with their character. This familiar spirit was not just a guardian or guide but a reflection of one's inner self. It could be a fierce bear, a wise owl, or a stealthy fox, embodying various aspects of one's personality. The demise of an individual often meant the end for their Fylgja—two entities intertwined in existence.

- **Hamingja:** An elusive and fascinating concept, hamingja intertwines luck, destiny, and ancestral spirit. It was more than just individual success; it was the culmination of family fate and history, passed down through generations, shaping and being shaped by one's actions and character. The continuing legacy of one's hamingja emphasized the deep ties between an individual and their ancestry.

The sagas offer fragmented glimpses into the Norse spiritual realm with their interwoven tapestry of life, death, and the interplay of these soul elements. But, like a mosaic missing tiles, the whole picture remains elusive. Legends of heroic figures like Baldr, who, despite his godly stature, finds himself in the dim realms of Hel, challenge simplistic interpretations of the Norse afterlife.

Documenting this intricate belief system proves challenging, given the scanty early sources and later Christian interpretations. Initially passed orally from skald to apprentice, Norse beliefs faced a transformation upon the arrival of Christianity and its chief instrument, the written word. The book introduced an element of permanence but rendered the dynamic oral traditions vulnerable to alterations by authors with different worldviews.

Death and the Afterlife in Norse Belief

In the rugged landscapes of the North, where harsh winters met brief, radiant summers, the Norse people developed a nuanced understanding of life and death. Each life was a tapestry of tales—of valor, love, betrayal, and kinship. *But what happens when the final thread is woven when the heart beats its last?* For the Norse, death was not an end but a transition to another realm of existence.

Valhalla

Valhalla, with its towering gates and magnificent halls, was not just an afterlife—it was an affirmation of a life lived with unparalleled courage. Its walls were said to be constructed from the shields of warriors, and its roof, thatched with golden shields, shimmered under the watchful eyes of the gods. Here, warriors found glory and purpose, preparing for a battle that would decide the fate of realms.

Inside the hall, warriors enthusiastically shared stories of their courage and adventures. They took turns recounting experiences from their lives, all while songs from famous singers played in the background. Each story, scar, and shout celebrated the unbreakable spirit of the Norse people.

A Day in Valhalla

Imagine waking up to the thrill of battle every dawn, clashing swords with fellow warriors, testing your valor, and sharpening your skills. But unlike the mortal world, defeat in Valhalla was not the end. At sundown, every wound would heal, every fallen warrior would rise, and the vast hall would transition from a battleground to a grand feasting arena.

It was here, amidst long tables laden with the finest meats and mead, that the Einherjar would celebrate. And watching over them with pride was Odin, for whom these brave souls were chosen protectors, destined to stand shoulder to shoulder with him during Ragnarök, the twilight of the gods.

Criteria for Entering Valhalla

The path to Valhalla was one of honor and bravery, and not all were destined to walk it. As battles raged in the mortal realm, the Valkyries swooped down from the skies on their majestic steeds. These maidens, acting on Odin's behalf, had a singular mission: to identify and select those who showcased exceptional valor.

It was not just about combat prowess; it was about the heart with which one fought, the unwavering spirit, the refusal to yield even when faced with overwhelming odds. Those chosen by the Valkyries were not just warriors—they were legends, and their legacy would never dim in Valhalla.

Hel

Beneath the sprawling branches and roots of Yggdrasil lies the enigmatic realm of Hel. Named after its ruler, Hel, the daughter of the trickster god Loki, this realm is often misunderstood due to its modern associations with the concept of *'Hell.'* However, to truly grasp its essence, one must look beyond contemporary misconceptions and delve into the ancient Norse understanding of death and the afterlife.

For the Norse, Hel was not a place of torment, fire, or eternal suffering, as it is often portrayed in later religious texts. Instead, it was a vast expanse of calm and solitude, a place where souls could find respite after the tribulations of life. The landscape of Hel was often depicted as somber, with vast plains, still waters, and dense mists, reflecting its nature as a realm of introspection and peace.

Hel, the ruler of this domain, was neither malevolent nor vengeful. With her body half-alive and half-deceased, she embodied the duality of existence and nonexistence. As a guardian of the departed, she ensured that souls in her realm were treated fairly and respected, providing them the tranquility they sought.

Criteria for Entering Hel

The criteria for entry into Hel were straightforward yet profound. While Valkyries chose the valiant warriors who died in battle for the great halls of Valhalla, Hel was the destination for most souls. Those who passed away due to old age, illness, or other natural causes were ushered into this realm.

Being directed to Hel was not seen as a lesser fate. The Norse recognized every life's inherent value and dignity, regardless of its end. While the valorous feats of warriors were celebrated with great fervor, the quiet perseverance of those who lived through the rhythms of daily life—farmers, artisans, mothers, and elders— was equally revered. Their journey to Hel was a testament to a life of resilience and grace, deserving of an eternity of peace.

In the gentle embrace of mists and silence, spirits could reunite with long-lost loved ones, reminisce about days gone by, or bask in the realm's serene stillness. It was a place of reflection where souls could ponder their mortal journeys, drawing wisdom from both joys and sorrows. Over time, many believed these spirits would guide and protect the living, their whispers carrying the accumulated wisdom of ages, serving as ethereal beacons for generations.

Runes

Runes are far more than just pretty etchings or symbols on stones. These ancient symbols, used by the Germanic people (including the Vikings), have fascinated scholars, spiritual seekers, and historians for centuries. Today, people often turn to runes for spiritual exploration, meditation, or divination. Many seek to understand the ancient wisdom of these symbols and connect with the energies of the Old Norse world. Delve deep into the world of runes and uncover their origins, meanings, and the magic they possess.

Origins

Imagine standing at the shores of ancient Scandinavia, the cold winds whipping around you and the Norse longships dotting the horizon. Among these hardy people, the runes were born as letters, symbols, and powerful magic tools.

The earliest runic inscriptions date back to around 150 AD. Runes were used by various Germanic tribes and later by the Norse. They were not just an alphabet but also held spiritual and mystical meanings.

The Runic Alphabet

Runes were not just scribbles. They were structured in a specific way, grouped into a futhark – akin to the modern 'alphabet.' The term *"futhark"* comes from the first six letters of the runic sequence: *F, U, P, A, R,* and *K.*

The Elder Futhark, the earliest and most well-known of the runic alphabets, consists of 24 characters. Named after the first six runes *(Fehu, Uruz, Thurisaz, Ansuz, Raidho,* and *Kenaz)*, this ancient system was the canvas on which much of the Norse lore was painted. These runes represented sounds for writing and held deeper esoteric meanings. Each rune was associated with gods, myths, natural elements, or philosophical concepts, turning written communication into spiritual expression. As time passed, variations like the Younger Futhark emerged with fewer characters and regional differences.

Meanings and Magic

In the dimly lit halls of the Viking Age, a seer might cast runes to predict the future, or a warrior might etch them onto his weapon for luck and power. Magic users believed they could channel its power by inscribing the right rune. Runes were used for divination, protection, attracting love, ensuring victory in battle, and more.

Each rune is not just a letter but a symbol infused with meaning and energy. Below is a concise overview of the associations of each rune in Futhark:

Fehu (ᚠ)

- **Gods or Mythological:** Associated with Freyja and Freyr, gods of fertility and prosperity.
- **Natural Elements:** Cattle, which were a sign of wealth in ancient times.
- **Concept:** This rune represents possessions, abundance, and success. It signifies wealth, not just in terms of money but also in success and prosperity in various aspects of life.

Uruz (ᚢ)

- **Gods or Mythological:** Often linked with the Æsir, the group of warrior gods, and Audhumla, the primordial cow from which the first beings were created.
- **Natural Elements:** Aurochs, a wild ox known for its strength and vitality.
- **Concept:** Uruz embodies raw strength, vitality, and untamed potential. It is about the primal force that drives growth, healing, and personal development.

Thurisaz (ᚦ)

- **Gods or Mythological:** This rune is deeply connected with Thor, the god of thunder and lightning, and the giants against whom he often fought.
- **Natural Elements:** Thorn or a giant's club, which can both harm and protect.
- **Concept:** Thurisaz represents a dual force that can be protective, defensive, and harmful if not approached with respect. It is also about boundaries, both setting them and respecting them.

Ansuz (ᚠ)

- **Gods or Mythological:** Ansuz is strongly associated with Odin, the all-father and god of wisdom, poetry, and war.
- **Natural Elements:** Breath, as in the breath of life or the spoken word.
- **Concept:** This rune represents communication, wisdom, and messages. It is about eloquence, advice, and guidance, often of a divine nature.

Raidho (ᚱ)

- **Gods or Mythological:** Not particularly linked to a specific god, but it encompasses the idea of the journeys that many gods and heroes underwent.
- **Natural Elements:** Wheel or chariot, symbolizing movement and cycles.
- **Concept:** Raidho is about journeys, both physical and spiritual. It is the rhythm of life, movement, travel, and lessons learned from experiences.

Kenaz (ᚲ)

- **Gods or Mythological:** Not associated with a specific god but is often linked to the knowledge possessed by the gods.
- **Natural Elements:** Torch, representing the light that dispels the darkness.
- **Concept:** Kenaz embodies enlightenment, knowledge, and learning. It is about the fire of creation and inspiration, the light that illuminates the unknown.

Guide to Rune Casting

To cast runes means to throw or draw a set of these symbols to divine answers to questions or discern the path ahead. Each rune drawn would be interpreted based on its inherent meaning and position relative to other runes. This practice was not random; it was an intimate conversation with the universe, seeking guidance and wisdom. Some practitioners used specific spreads or patterns while casting, much like tarot readings, to gain insights into various aspects of life. Whether seeking knowledge about love, war, or fate, runes were the voice of the gods and spirits, offering counsel and foresight. If you are interested, here's a guide on rune casting.

1. **Preparing Your Mind and Space**
   Before any spiritual endeavor, approach with the right mindset. Rune casting is no different.
   - **Clear your mind.** Take a few moments to meditate. Calm your thoughts and focus on your intention.
   - **Prepare the space:** Choose a quiet space free from distractions. Some practitioners like to light candles or incense to purify the area or play soft, ambient music to set the tone.

2. **Formulate Your Question**
   Every conversation needs a topic, and your question serves this purpose in rune casting.
   - **Be clear and precise:** The more specific your question, the clearer the guidance you might receive.
   - **Avoid yes or no questions:** Instead of asking, *"Will I get the job?"* consider *"What should I be aware of regarding this job opportunity?"*

3. **Choose Your Rune Set**
   The tools of the trade, your rune set, can be made of various materials, each carrying its energy.

- ○ **Materials:** Runes can be crafted from wood, stone, crystal, or bone. Choose a set that resonates with you.
- ○ **Personal Connection:** Some believe a gifted set or one you make yourself can be more powerful. Feel the energy of the runes and develop a bond with them.

4. **The Casting Method**
How you cast the runes can affect the message they convey.
- ○ **Random Draw:** Focus on your question and draw one or more runes from a bag.
- ○ **Spread Casting:** Scatter the runes onto a cloth or table. The runes landing face up are then interpreted, considering their position relative to each other and the question posed.

5. **Interpretation**
Now, the magic unfolds. The runes have spoken, but understanding them requires intuition and knowledge.
- ○ **Know each rune's meaning:** Familiarize yourself with the symbolism of each rune. This is the foundation of interpretation.
- ○ **Context matters:** How runes relate to each other in a spread can alter or deepen their meanings.
- ○ **Trust your intuition:** Sometimes, the runes may evoke a feeling or thought unrelated to their traditional meaning. This is the universe speaking to you in its language; listen to it.

6. **Closing the Session**
Just as you prepared the space, it is essential to close the session, sealing the energies and showing gratitude.
- ○ **Thank the runes:** A simple gesture of gratitude to the runes and the universe can close your session. This respects the wisdom they have shared.

o **Cleanse your set:** Over time, your runes might pick up different energies. Regularly cleansing them (using moonlight, smudging, or other methods) ensures they remain a pure channel for guidance.

CHAPTER 8

NORSE MYTHOLOGY IN HISTORICAL CONTEXT

The turbulent seas of the Viking Age were alive with mighty warriors, intricate longships, and tales of gods and monsters echoing through time. The bustling docksides of Scandinavia teemed with merchants bartering with distant goods and sailors recounting stories of uncharted lands. While many know of Thor's legendary hammer or Odin's wise raven, the tapestry of Norse mythology is vast and interconnected. This chapter embarks on Norse voyages reaching the furthest corners of medieval Europe and beyond. As Norse explorers intertwined with various cultures, their stories and traditions began to evolve. The crossroads of faith emerged as the thunderous gods of the North encountered the solemn cross of Christianity. The coexistence of these beliefs, the transformations they underwent, and their eventual convergence is a tale of wonder and intrigue.

The Viking Age

From the late 8th to the early 11th century, the Viking Age marked a pivotal period in European history. Originating in the Scandinavian regions—what is now Denmark, Norway, and Sweden—these seafaring Norse people ventured far and wide. *But who exactly were the Vikings?* Contrary to some popular imagery of horned helmets and relentless plundering, the Vikings were traders, explorers, and settlers. Their journeys began not out of sheer wanderlust but primarily due to overpopulation and the search for new trading partners and territories.

Voyages

With their iconic dragon-headed prows, the Vikings' sturdy long-ships allowed them to travel vast distances. These were both tools of war and symbols of exploration. These vessels, crafted expertly from wood and iron, were designed for the open sea and shallow rivers. This allowed the Vikings to explore further and with more versatility than others. They reached as far east as Russia, forming trade routes down the Volga River and as far south as the Mediterranean, mingling with the Byzantines. Their travels even took them as far west as Newfoundland, making them among the first Europeans to set foot in North America—predating Columbus by nearly 500 years!

Influence and Interactions with Other Cultures

The tales of Norse mythology do not just paint a picture of gods and giants; they echo the spirit of the Viking people, adventurers who set out to explore, trade, and sometimes raid. Their ventures led them to distant shores, intertwining their fates with numerous cultures and leaving an indelible mark in global history.

British Isles

The late 8th century witnessed the Norse beginning their raids on the British Isles, an era punctuated with moments like the sacking of the Lindisfarne monastery in 793 AD. As the years rolled by, the dynamics shifted. What had commenced as aggressive raids eventually transitioned into settlements. In regions like York, renamed Jorvik by the Norse, they integrated their tales of Odin, Thor, and Yggdrasil with Celtic and Anglo-Saxon folklore.

Russia and the Eastern Expansion

Venturing into present-day Russia and Ukraine, Norse traders, commonly called the Varangians, established robust trade networks along the Volga River. These trade routes soon gave birth to settlements and a deep-rooted integration with the Slavic populace. As the Norse assimilated with Slavic communities, there was an evident cross-cultural exchange.

The Mediterranean and Byzantine Contact

Some Norse adventurers traveled southward, reaching the vibrant city of Constantinople, now known as Istanbul. Their reputation was not limited to trading; their combat prowess was so renowned that they became the Varangian Guard, tasked with protecting Byzantine emperors.

The North Atlantic and Exploration of Iceland, Greenland, and Vinland

The spirit of exploration led Norse navigators, like Erik the Red and his progeny, Leif Erikson, to the shores of Iceland and Greenland. These new colonies burgeoned as crucial centers of Norse culture and mythos. Their exploration itch did not stop there; journeying further west, they found parts of North America, naming it Vinland. Even though these settlements did not last long, they introduced elements of Norse mythology to the indigenous tribes, laying down early roots of cross-cultural interactions.

Normand

The Norse journey also touched the coasts of present-day France. Notably, a Norse leader named Rollo secured territories that evolved into what many may recognize as Normandy. This marked the Norse's deeper dive into the broader European political and cultural landscape.

Christianization

The story of Christianity's introduction to Norse society showcases a blending of traditions, a melding of old and new beliefs, and a significant cultural shift. It was not a simple replacement process but a journey of adaptation, compromise, and an intertwining of cultures. Two pivotal aspects stand out in navigating the vast shift from paganism to Christianity: *Syncretism* and *Conversion Strategies*.

Syncretism

When two cultures intersect, they do not always clash; often, they intertwine. Such was the case during the Christianization of Norse lands. Rather than a tectonic shift where one belief system eclipsed the other, there was a melding and weaving of stories, symbols, and practices. This interlacing embodies syncretism, where religious or cultural traditions find common ground and fuse.

As the Norse embraced Christianity, they did not discard their identity. Instead, they wove it into the new religion they were adopting. It was not a replacement but a reimagination. Through syncretism, the Norse ensured that while their beliefs evolved, their roots remained ever-present, grounding them amidst change. Listed below are examples of how they did this.

Euhemerization of Norse Myths

Euhemerization is when real historical events are turned into myths or when gods from ancient stories are seen as actual historical people whose divine characteristics were added later. As Christianity spread through Scandinavia, many Norse myths underwent euhemerization.

One of the prime examples is Snorri Sturluson's *"Prose Edda."* While Snorri's goal may have been to preserve the old stories, his rendition often interpreted the Norse gods as historical heroes rather than deities. Odin, for instance, was presented not as a god but as a human chieftain who acquired a divine status over time due to his remarkable deeds. Placing such figures in a tangible historical context made these stories more aligned with Christian narratives, where divine events often had historical grounding.

Parallels and Analogies

There were striking similarities between certain Norse and Christian stories that eased the transition for many. Consider the tale of Odin hanging himself from Yggdrasil for nine nights to gain knowledge. This act of self-sacrifice and suffering bore resemblances to the crucifixion of Christ. To the Norse, the two stories could serve as parallel tales of sacrifice for the greater good or enlightenment.

Another example lies in the tale of Ragnarok, where the world undergoes significant destruction followed by a rebirth. This narrative parallels Christian concepts of the Apocalypse and the subsequent emergence of a new paradise.

Artistic Fusion in Architecture

Beyond myths and stories, syncretism was visibly prominent in art and architecture. Churches constructed during this transitional phase bore witness to this fusion. During this transition period, churches showed signs of merging two cultures. Norwegian churches are a prime example. While mainly built for Christian worship, they incorporated designs similar to Viking ships and classic Norse artwork, like detailed woodwork, dragonhead gables, and decorative doorways. It is as though they blended the Norse spirit with Christian symbols in their construction.

Conversion Strategies

Understanding the profound cultural and spiritual significance of Norse paganism, Christian missionaries were cautious in introducing Christianity to the Norse people. They recognized that forceful attempts at conversion could lead to outright rejection or resistance to Christianity. Instead, these missionaries opted for subtler, more integrative strategies to intertwine Christian teachings with established Norse beliefs and customs.

Christian missionaries, aiming to convert the Norse pagans, adopted a multi-faceted approach to introduce and spread Christianity. Recognizing the deep-rooted beliefs and traditions of the Norse people, the missionaries tailored their strategies to blend the familiar with the new. Here's a brief outline of some of these conversion strategies:

Integration of Holidays

One such strategy was to introduce Christian holidays during the same periods as pagan celebrations. Yule, a Norse pagan festival, was celebrated around the same time as Christmas. By aligning Christian celebrations with traditional Norse festivals, missionaries could promote Christian beliefs while allowing the Norse to celebrate at a familiar time.

Adaptation of Symbols

Another significant compromise was the introduction of Christian symbols alongside pagan ones. The cross, a symbol of Christianity, was often worn alongside Thor's hammer, Mjölnir, showing a simultaneous reverence for both beliefs.

The cross is one of the most recognized symbols worldwide, representing the Christian faith and the crucifixion of Jesus Christ. To early Christians in Norse territories, wearing the cross was a sign of faith and a protective charm, much like how pagan symbols were worn for protection and blessing.

Mjölnir, the hammer of Thor, was a potent symbol in Viking society. Representing strength, protection, and authority, it was a common amulet worn by the Norse. The hammer symbolizes Thor's role as a protector of mankind, his power to challenge the giants, and his authority over thunder and lightning.

Wearing the cross and Mjölnir simultaneously was more profound than a mere fashion choice. It was a statement. It represented a respect for traditions, an acknowledgment of the new faith, and a personal compromise in a changing world.

Moreover, this dual adornment allowed individuals to navigate the social intricacies of a society in flux. In areas where Christianity had a stronger foothold, showcasing the cross was a sign of alignment with the new order. Meanwhile, Mjölnir was a symbol of heritage and continuity in areas still deeply rooted in Norse traditions.

Political Alliances

The conversion of the Norse was not just a spiritual endeavor but also had political dimensions. Missionaries often understood the hierarchical nature of Norse societies and knew that aligning with the political elite could be pivotal in mass conversions. By converting kings, chieftains, and other local rulers, missionaries ensured that Christianity had the endorsement of the highest echelons of society. Once a leader adopted the new faith, it became the de facto religion of the court and, by extension, its subjects. Kings like Olaf Tryggvason and Olaf Haraldsson did not just adopt Christianity; they became champions of it, enforcing its teachings in their domains and using their political and military might to quash pagan practices.

Building Churches on Sacred Sites

This strategy was both symbolic and practical. By constructing Christian churches on or near locations considered sacred in Norse paganism, missionaries sent a clear message: Christianity was here to stay and was taking the place of the old gods. From a more practical perspective, the Norse people were already accustomed to visiting these sites for spiritual and communal activities. Therefore, building churches on these sites ensured that they continued to be centers of communal gathering. Over time, as people attended these churches, the lines between pagan and Christian practices began to blur, and the new faith became deeply rooted in the societal fabric.

Preservation of Norse Myths

When diving into the vast sea of Norse mythology, one cannot help but wonder: *How have these tales of gods, giants, and legendary heroes endured through centuries, especially in a time where oral traditions were dominant?* The intricate preservation of Norse myths depicts dedication, reverence, and a deep-seated desire to keep cultural memories alive.

The Norse integrated mythology and history, often blending mythological events and characters into their historical accounts without distinguishing between the two. This blend offers a captivating perspective on how the Norse viewed their world: a realm where gods, giants, and mortals could intersect, and mythological events could influence historical outcomes. When delving into the ways the Norse myths have been preserved, three pivotal aspects stand out, providing a structured tapestry of tales, traditions, and historical recounts: *The Eddas, the chronicling of oral traditions,* and *the sagas.*

The Eddas

If one were to consider the cornerstones of Norse mythology documentation, the Eddas would stand tall. These ancient Icelandic texts serve as primary sources of mythological and heroic content.

The Poetic Edda, sometimes called the Elder Edda, is a compilation of ancient poetic narratives. These poems cover a range of tales, from the creation of the world to its eventual destruction in Ragnarök, and provide invaluable insights into Norse cosmology.

Then there is The Prose Edda, crafted by the historian Snorri Sturluson. This work, also termed the Younger Edda, not only narrates myths but serves as a guide on poetic methodology, ensuring the continuation of traditional Norse poetic forms.

Chronicling Oral Traditions

Before the written preservation of myths, stories were shared orally and passed down from generation to generation. These tales were recounted in gatherings, during long winter nights, or in celebratory feasts. But, with the onset of Christianization, there was a pressing need to document these tales as oral traditions started to wane and written forms gained prominence.

Recording these oral narratives was more than a mere clerical exercise. It was an endeavor of cultural preservation to ensure that the tales of gods like Odin, Thor, and Freyja were not lost in the sands of time.

Sagas

While the Eddas are rich in mythological content, the sagas are narratives celebrating historical figures, legendary heroes, and even ordinary people. These prose histories detailed events that supposedly occurred in the Viking Age, often weaving in elements of myth and magic.

A prominent example is The Saga of the Volsungs, a legendary saga that narrates the tale of the Völsung dynasty. This saga is particularly significant as it intertwines historical heroes with mythological elements, blurring the lines between fact and fantasy.

Other Texts

While texts like the Eddas and Sagas form the backbone of Norse mythological preservation, the myths pulsed through more than ink on parchment. Their essence was engraved on stones, recited in poetic melodies, and illustrated on the artifacts of daily life. These mediums breathed life into the legends, keeping them vibrant and relevant.

Preserving Norse myths was never a passive act. It was a dynamic interplay of recitation, illustration, and celebration. The tales were not only reserved for special occasions; they were a part of life, love, and even death. The Norse ensured their legends would endure through poetry, stone, and art, echoing their beliefs and values across time and terrain.

Skaldic Poetry

Composed by skalds or court poets, these intricate verses were crafted to honor kings and heroes and often intertwined historical events with mythological themes. The poems, with their kennings *(poetic metaphors)* and complex structures, not only preserved myths but also showcased the linguistic and creative prowess of the Norse people.

Runestones

Across the Scandinavian landscape, large stones etched with runes stand tall. These runestones, often commissioned as memorials for the deceased, carry inscriptions that narrate deeds of valor, journeys, or historical events. But interspersed with these are references to gods, legendary figures, and mythological events. Every runestone is a page from a grand Norse narrative, with tales of mortals and gods standing side by side.

Archaeological Imprints

Venture into a museum showcasing Viking artifacts, and Norse mythology comes alive in the most tactile manner. From petroglyphs illustrating the might of Thor to intricate jewelry depicting the World Tree, Yggdrasil—the myths found their way into art and daily objects. Helmets adorned with motifs from the myths, ship burials with references to the voyage to the afterlife, and even simple household items bearing the symbols of gods and creatures from the myths—these artifacts testify to the deep-rooted influence of Norse mythology in everyday Viking life.

CHAPTER 9

THE REVIVAL OF NORSE PAGAN PRACTICES

Once upon a time, in the frosty realms of Scandinavia, tales of powerful gods, wily giants, and brave warriors echoed through the valleys. These stories, forgotten by many as time passed, were the lifeblood of the Vikings and their ancestors. *But what if these tales are not just dusty relics of a bygone era?*

You will begin with rediscovering old roots. As you dive deep into the sands of time, you will unearth ancient relics and texts that whisper the stories of Odin, Freyja, and their kin. The role of archaeology and academia cannot be understated in this grand rediscovery. But like any treasure hunt, there are twists and turns. Modern interpretations clash with historical realities, creating a tapestry of old and new. Next, you will step into the world of the Modern Ásatrú Movement. Here, pioneers breathe life into old rituals, blóts, and celebrations, forging a vibrant path called Heathenry. This path is not without its thorns, however. Challenges, controversies, and debates ensue as ancient beliefs meet modern mindsets. Yet, the allure of the Norse gods is undeniable. They are not confined to the North anymore. Pop culture has played its part, with epic sagas unfolding on screens, books, and art. From Thor's might in blockbuster films to the nuanced portrayals in literature, these gods are more alive than ever. And so, you see a global resonance, a melding of old Norse beliefs with the beat of today's world.

Rediscovering Old Roots

Imagine a treasure chest. But instead of gold and jewels, this chest is filled with old parchments, stories, and relics that can breathe life into myths buried in the sands of time. The allure of Norse mythology is a bit like that; it calls you back to a past that seems at once mysterious and strangely familiar. It is like a distant echo we have all heard but cannot quite place. Here are various dimensions of how people reconnect with Norse Mythology in the present day.

Written Words

At the heart of rediscovery is the written word. Considering that the Viking Age was more than a thousand years ago, you might think these ancient stories would be hard to come by. Surprisingly, as you have learned in the previous chapter, that is untrue. While the Vikings were not prolific writers, later generations—especially medieval Christian monks—were fascinated enough to pen down these tales in works like the Poetic Edda and the Prose Edda.

Physical Relics

Physical relics and artifacts offer another layer of insight. For example, runestones share condensed stories, often describing heroic deeds or significant events. Some even invoke the gods themselves, like a runestone from Sweden that mentions Thor and asks for his protection. Another compelling find is the Mjöl-nir amulets—small hammer-shaped trinkets symbolizing Thor's hammer. These have been discovered in various parts of the Viking world, illustrating the god's widespread appeal and the deep-rooted belief in his protective powers.

Modern-day Seekers

This rediscovery is not just the work of dusty academics in ivory towers. Enchanted by these old stories, regular people are picking up the torch. They are not just reading about Thor and Odin but bringing them into their daily lives. These modern-day seekers are exploring their ancestral paths in a variety of ways. Some are studying Old Norse, the language of the Vikings, to read the Eddas in their original form. Others visit ancient sites like the temple at Uppsala in Sweden or immerse themselves in Viking festivals like the one in Jorvik, England.

Fusing Stories with Identity

What is remarkable is how these stories, once rediscovered, begin to take on their own life. They are not just dusty tales to be archived in a museum or skimmed over in a book. Instead, they become a part of people's identity. In Iceland, for example, a growing Ásatrú community celebrates the old gods and practices rituals that have roots in the Norse past. The same holds for many in Scandinavia and places as far-flung as the United States and Australia.

Rediscovering these old roots is not merely an exercise in nostalgia. It engages with a rich, complex past with much to teach us. Through the Eddas, runestones, and the passion of modern-day seekers, these ancient stories and beliefs are experiencing a revival. And as we'll see in the upcoming sections, this revival is far from a straightforward journey. It involves walking a tightrope between historical accuracy and modern interpretation, between ancient wisdom and present-day relevance.

As you venture further into this chapter, remember that these are not just the stories of gods and giants but of us all. They ask the big questions about life, love, sacrifice, and what it means to be human. By rediscovering these old roots, we also find new pathways to explore these timeless themes. We are reconnecting with a past that feels foreign and incredibly close to home. And in doing so, we are breathing new life into the old gods, allowing them to walk among us once more.

The Modern Ásatrú Movement

In a world filled with technological advancements, where traditions often get lost in the noise of innovation, an ancient heartbeat is re-emerging. This heartbeat, resonating from the rugged landscapes of ancient Scandinavia, pulses through the Modern Ásatrú Movement, reviving connections with gods once revered.

Origins and Pioneers of the Revival

One must enter the 1970s' global context to truly understand the revival's birth. Profound societal shifts marked this period: *the Civil Rights Movement, anti-war protests,* and *the feminist wave.* Amidst these, the Space Age and technological advancements meant humanity was simultaneously looking skyward and inward, exploring new frontiers while questioning age-old beliefs. There was a palpable sense of yearning—a desire for something genuine, meaningful, and rooted in authenticity.

Iceland, an island deeply rooted in age-old legends and closely tied to the rhythms of nature, stood out amidst the changing times. The nation maintained a deep connection with its ancestral stories, which resonated in the whispers of its people, the winds across its terrains, and its very identity. However, with the advance of modernization, there arose a concern that these cherished tales might be overshadowed, reduced to mere historical sidenotes.

Sveinbjörn Beinteinsson

Enter Sveinbjörn Beinteinsson, a man who wore many hats—a farmer, a poet, and a deep believer in the old ways. He recognized the growing disconnection between the modern Icelandic individual and their mythological roots. But more than just recognizing this, Beinteinsson decided to act. In 1972, he founded the Ásatrúarfélagið.

The organization is not only about worship; it was a movement, an institution aiming to integrate the Norse gods' wisdom into contemporary life. Under Beinteinsson's leadership, the Ásatrúarfélagið facilitated ceremonies, blóts *(ritualistic offerings to the gods)*, and educational initiatives. These were not just hollow rituals; they were, and remain, heartfelt expressions of faith, love, and reverence for the old ways.

A Legacy Beyond Tales

What set the Ásatrúarfélagið apart from the entire revival movement was its insistence on viewing the Norse pantheon not as mere characters in tales but as guides. Odin was not just the one-eyed god of wisdom; he symbolized the quest for knowledge and the sacrifices one makes. Thor was not merely the hammer-wielding deity; he embodied strength, resilience, and the protective nature humans often exhibit. More than a goddess of love, Freyja represented the myriad emotions and passions humans grapple with.

This modern yet deeply rooted perspective helped countless individuals navigate the complexities of the 20th century, grounding them in principles that had withstood the test of time. It was a renaissance of belief, an intertwining of ancient wisdom with modern sensibilities, and it started, quite fittingly, in a land where the gods had once freely roamed.

Challenges and Controversies

A movement resurrecting age-old beliefs inevitably faces challenges. Authenticity is a recurring question: How accurate are modern interpretations? Moreover, as Ásatrú gained prominence, some factions sought to intertwine it with nationalistic or exclusionary ideologies. This distortion has been a cause of concern for many genuine practitioners who advocate a more inclusive and spiritually pure approach to Ásatrú.

The allure of Ásatrú is not limited to Scandinavia. Its influence has reached the Americas, Europe, and the Southern Hemisphere. These communities comprise not just those with Norse ancestry but individuals drawn to the faith's core principles. This global embrace stands as testimony to the universal themes and values embedded in the tales and tenets of Ásatrú.

Blending Norse Beliefs with Modern Values

While reading the chapters of this book, it is becoming evident that Norse Mythology is more than just ancient stories; it is a living, breathing tradition that continues to shape and inspire its followers in the 21st century.

Navigating through the modern world with its ever-evolving values can sometimes feel overwhelming. Ancient tales and beliefs, such as those of the Norse, can offer a grounding perspective. This section uncovers the intertwining of Norse beliefs with today's values, exploring how the moral compass of legendary figures can guide contemporary choices and how the Norse's respect for nature can inspire environmental endeavors.

Moral Compass of Yore

In today's fast-paced world, with its relentless stream of innovations and momentary fascinations, there is a tangible thirst for enduring values. With its rich tapestry of tales and characters, Norse mythology offers a wellspring of wisdom to quench this thirst. Listed below are the specific values you can draw from these ancient narratives.

- **Integrity:** Odin's unquenchable thirst for knowledge made him sacrifice an eye at Mímir's well. This was not a mere transaction but a deep commitment to a higher goal. From this, we learn that integrity goes beyond honesty. It speaks to staying true to one's convictions and being consistent with our principles, even when faced with personal costs.
- **Courage:** The tales of Thor brim with lessons of bravery. His confrontations with giants and serpents were not just demonstrations of physical strength. They encapsulate the essence of courage: facing fears, standing up against towering odds, and defending core values. In Thor's dauntless endeavors, we see reflections on our battles and the importance of championing the causes dear to us.
- **Perseverance:** The Norse gods, fully aware of the looming apocalypse of Ragnarök, provide a profound lesson in perseverance. Their unwavering determination in the face of impending doom underscores the significance of tenacity. It is a powerful reminder that the path we tread and the choices we make have value, irrespective of pre-ordained outcomes.
- **Wisdom:** Odin's ceaseless journey for wisdom, from sacrificing his eye to enduring pain on Yggdrasil to acquire the runes, serves as a testament to the importance of continuous learning. His dedication reminds us of the depth

and breadth of wisdom and the sacrifices one might make in its pursuit.

- **Loyalty and Brotherhood:** The intricate web of relationships in Norse mythology, exemplified by the bond between brothers Odin, Vili, and Vé, or the unity of the Aesir and Vanir post-truce, shines a light on the sanctity of loyalty. These relationships underscore the bedrock of trust, the strength derived from alliances, and the power of standing by one's comrades.

Environmental Reverence

Modern society is coming to terms with the importance of nature, and here too, Norse beliefs have wisdom to offer. The ancient Norse held a profound respect for the environment. Consider Yggdrasil, the World Tree, whose roots and branches intertwined realms. It was not just a mythological concept but a representation of nature's interconnectivity and significance. Today, as we rally around environmental causes, there is inspiration to be drawn from this age-old veneration of the natural world.

Pop Culture's Role in Norse Resurgence

From Thor's thunderous roars to Loki's cunning, the silver screen has played a pivotal role in reintroducing Norse mythology to the masses. With their grandiose portrayals, films have made gods relatable, turning them from distant deities to familiar faces. One cannot help but cheer for Thor as he navigates the challenges of both Asgard and Earth or be intrigued by the complex machinations of Loki.

While movies offer visual spectacles, literature provides depth. Acclaimed authors like Neil Gaiman have delved into Norse mythology, weaving intricate tales that captivate readers, making them yearn for more. Through these books, a new generation encounters the Norse pantheon, not as archaic tales but as living narratives with layers of meaning.

The digital realm, especially video games, has become an unexpected bastion of Norse lore. Games transport players to immersive worlds where they can walk alongside gods, confront mythical beasts, and grapple with themes of fate, honor, and sacrifice.

CONCLUSION

The enduring allure of Norse mythology stems from the profound questions it explores. As one journey through these ancient tales, engaging characters and spectacular events are encountered. But beyond the battles, betrayals, and triumphs lies a deeper resonance. These myths hold up a mirror, reminding you of hopes, fears, and purpose in the grandeur of existence.

In previous chapters, the various facets that make Norse lore so captivating were explored. From the mystical origins of Yggdrasil to the devastating twilight of the gods, these myths present a nuanced worldview. The virtues and flaws of the gods were evident, reflecting broader universal themes. Concepts of fate, destiny, and free will were intertwined in every interaction.

By documenting the expansion and transformation of Norse beliefs, the intricate interplay between myths and history was revealed. The Vikings emerged not just as warriors but also as traders, explorers, and settlers. Their contact with diverse cultures shaped and reshaped their myths. This interplay conveyed a significant insight: *Myths continually reinvent themselves by absorbing varied influences.*

The resurgence of Norse paganism highlights the eternal truths embedded in these stories. Through practices like the Ásatrú movement, followers blend age-old wisdom with contemporary life. This revival stands as evidence of the enduring insights found within myths. Like precious gems hidden beneath time's sands, they merely require unveiling to showcase their timeless luster.

As you end this voyage, the ultimate takeaway is clear: Myths are more than entertainment; they are teachers and healers. In Odin's eternal search for knowledge, Thor's tireless defense of order, and Loki's delight in chaos, purpose, and meaning are found. These stories are existential maps guiding you through the labyrinth of creation.

So when thunder rumbles, or one gazes up at the vast expanse of stars, remember that the Norse myths are not limited to history books. They are alive, intricately woven into the fabric of our collective consciousness. Their enchantment lingers in every heart, ready to stir the soul. While mainstream media offers glimpses, often adorned with creative liberties, it is essential to dive deeper, seeking authentic sources to truly appreciate this rich tapestry. The true magic of Norse mythology awaits those willing to delve beneath the surface. As you close this book, may the tales you have encountered inspire you to continually seek out and cherish the genuine depth and richness of Norse legends.

REFERENCES

Charles River Editors. (2017). Ragnarok: The Origins and History of the Apocalypse in Norse Mythology. CreateSpace Independent Publishing Platform.

Crossley-Holland, K. (2017). Norse Myths: Tales of Odin, Thor and Loki. Candlewick Press.

Facts On File, Incorporated. (2009). Norse Mythology A to Z. Infobase Publishing.

Garrison, T. (2023). Norse Mythology: From the Origin of the Universe to Ragnarok. Explore the Nine Worlds among Legends, Gods, Heroes, and Myths of the North. Tom Garrison.

Hansen, D. (2017). Norse Mythology: Tales of Norse Gods, Heroes, Beliefs, Rituals and the Viking Legacy. Createspace Independent Publishing Platform.

Hayes, B. (2019). Norse Mythology: A Concise Guide to the Gods, Heroes, Sagas, Rituals, and Beliefs of Norse Mythology. Vincent Noot.

Hermann, P. (2018). Handbook of Pre-Modern Nordic Memory Studies: Interdisciplinary Approaches. Walter de Gruyter GmbH & Co KG.

Herman, A. (2021). The Viking Heart: How Scandinavians Conquered the World. Houghton Mifflin Harcourt.

Kirch, A. B. (1914). The Influence of Geography Upon Primitive Religions. University of Wisconsin--Madison.

Litchfield, M. E. (1890). The Nine Worlds: Stories from Norse Mythology. Ginn.

Long, S. (2015). Odin: The Viking Allfather. Bloomsbury Publishing.

McCoy, D. (2016). The Viking Spirit: An Introduction to Norse Mythology and Religion. CreateSpace Independent Publishing Platform.

Ogden, D. (2013). Drakon: Dragon Myth and Serpent Cult in the Greek and Roman Worlds. OUP Oxford.

Welch, L. C. (2001). Goddess of the North: A Comprehensive Exploration of the Norse Godesses, from Antiquity to the Modern Age. Weiser Books.

EXCLUSIVE BONUSES

Dear Reader,

I am thrilled to present to you a collection of five specially curated bonuses that accompany our exploration into the enchanting realm of Norse mythology. These bonuses are designed to deepen your understanding and enhance your journey through the mystical and legendary worlds of ancient myths.

- **Bonus 1 - Legends Intertwined: Exploring the Myths of Norse, Egyptian, and Greek Pantheons**
  Dive into the fascinating interconnections between Norse, Egyptian, and Greek mythologies. This bonus offers a comparative study, highlighting the similarities and differences in themes, deities, and mythological tales across these rich and diverse pantheons.

- **Bonus 2 - Hidden Beasts of the North: Unveiling the Lesser-Known Creatures of Norse Mythology**
  Discover the mysterious and often overlooked creatures that roam the landscapes of Norse legends. From forest spirits to sea monsters, this guide brings to light the intriguing beings that have remained in the shadows of more famous mythological figures.

- **Bonus 3 - Shadows of Asgard: Uncovering the Lesser-Known Characters of Norse Mythology**
  Meet the lesser-known but equally fascinating characters of Norse mythology. This bonus delves into the stories and roles of figures who have played significant, yet often underappreciated, roles in the tapestry of Norse myths.

- **Bonus 4 - Deciphering the Past: A Beginner's Guide to Elder Futhark Runes**
  Embark on a journey to understand the ancient script of the Norse - the Elder Futhark runes. This guide provides beginners with an easy-to-follow introduction to rune meanings, historical context, and their use in divination and inscriptions.

- **Bonus 5 - Ancestral Webs of the Norse Pantheon: A Chart of Prominent Mythological Figures**
  Navigate the complex lineage and relationships of the Norse gods and goddesses with an intricately designed chart. This visual guide helps you understand the familial ties and connections between the major figures of Norse mythology.

How to Access Your Bonuses:

Scan the QR Code Below: Simply use your phone's camera or a QR code reader to scan the code, and you'll be directed straight to the bonus content.

Visit the Link: Access these enriching resources by visiting this link https://bit.ly/Borgerson-NM

Embark on this captivating journey through the myths and legends of the Norse world. I hope these bonuses will not only complement your reading experience but also leave you with a deeper appreciation for the rich tapestry of Norse mythology.

Warm regards,

Magnus Borgerson

Printed in Great Britain
by Amazon

46547735R00079